EE HOW MANY 'SHEET GHOSTS' YOU CAN SPOT HIDDEN IN THIS PICT
THE HAUNTED WOOD.
f you can only spot up to ten, then you obviously don't believe in ghosts. If you
ou could still find yourself being haunted, but if you can see twenty or more, no
up on you!
GW01607398
95p

FUSS POT
MABEL SMITH HAS BEEN ELECTED CAPTAIN OF THE SCHOOL HOCKEY TEAM!
WHAAT?

HOW DARE YOU NOT ELECT ME! I SHALL FUSS AND FUSS UNTIL YOU DO! RANT! RAGE!
OH, NO! WE AGREE!

SO...
YOUR CAPTAIN'S HOLDING UP THE MATCH! WONDER WHAT'S KEEPING HER?
WE CAN GUESS! GROAN!

AND...
I MUST LOOK MY FUSSY BEST...EVEN FOR A HOCKEY GAME!
PSSSS!
YOUR TAXI'S ARRIVED, FUSS POT... THE LIMOUSINE ONE! SIGH!

HERE SHE COMES AT LAST!
I'M FUSSY ABOUT ARRIVING IN STYLE!

SALUTE YOUR CAPTAIN, TEAM! I'M FUSSY ABOUT YOU SHOWING ME THE PROPER RESPECT!
MAYBE WE CAN GET STARTED NOW!

OOH! THERE'S A BIG CROWD! HOPE MY HAIR'S STILL IN PLACE!
SHE'S LET THE BALL GO TO THE OTHER SIDE!
PAT!
PAT!

I'M FUSSY ABOUT MY APPEARANCE! BETTER MANICURE MY NAILS, TOO!
YOURS, FUSS POT... UH?
SCRAPE!

NOT FORGETTING MY TEETH MIGHT NEED AN EXTRA BRUSH!
OH, NO! SHE'S LET THEM SCORE A GOAL!
SCRUB!

FINALLY...
THE GAME'S OVER AND I'M AS SPRUCE AS EVER! BUT YOU MUCKY LOT BETTER NOT CHAIR ME ON YOUR SHOULDERS... I'M FUSSY ABOUT SPOILING MY CLOTHES!
GRRR!

THERE'S NOTHING TO CHAIR YOU FOR! WE LOST 28-NIL! SCRAG HER!
EEEEEK! I SHALL RESIGN! I-I... HEEEELP!

Little Devil

THEY DID IT, MISTER! DON'T LET THEM GIVE YOU THE "SLIP" AGAIN!
OOER!
GRRR!

HO, HO! NOW THEY'LL BE FOR IT!
SEETHE!
GOT YOU!

YIPPEE! A DOUBLE WHACKING!
JAB!
NOW I'LL GIVE YOU TWO A FEW BRUISES...!

RUMBLE! RUMBLE!
LOOK OUT, MISTER! HE GAVE US THE BANANA SKIN!
JERK!
IS THAT SO..?
YERK! WHAT'VE I DONE

ROLL!
GRR! LEMME AT 'IM!
RUMBLE!
HELP!

TOSS!
CLAW!
TEE, HEE! WE'VE GOT LOADS OF FRUIT, THANKS TO LITTLE DEVIL!
GULP! I'VE REALLY UPSET THE APPLE-CART, THIS TIME!

WANDA
OF THE
SUPER SEVEN

HELP, SUPER SEVEN! BULLY BRIGGS IS LOOKING FOR ME!
OH, DEAR! THERE'S ONLY ME HERE, JIMMY — BUT I'LL COME AND HELP YOU...!

I HOPE I GET TO JIMMY BEFORE BULLY BRIGGS FINDS HIM...!
VROOM!
THE SUPER 7 MOBILE

I'M HERE, JIMMY! ANY SIGN OF BRIGGS?
N-NOT YET, WANDA!
SUPER 7

HAW, HAW! HERE I AM! THANKS FOR TAKING ME TO HIM, WANDA! I KNEW HE'D CALL THE SUPER SEVEN HUT!
GASP! BRIGGS WAS HIDING IN THE SEVENMOBILE ALL THE TIME!
TAP! TAP!
ACE BUILDERS LTD.
SUPER 7 MOBILE

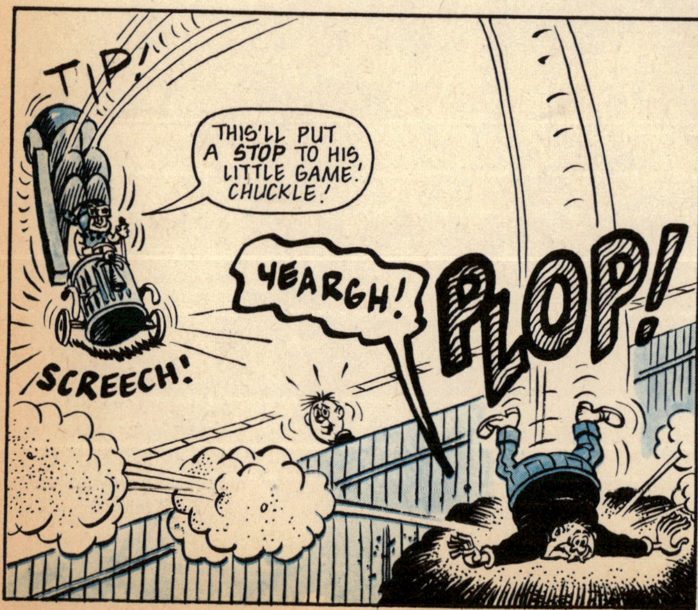
TIP!
THIS'LL PUT A STOP TO HIS LITTLE GAME! CHUCKLE!
SCREECH!
YEARGH!
PLOP!

HELP! BRIGGS WILL BE REALLY ANGRY AFTER THAT! I'D BETTER HIDE!
HEY! COME BACK, JIMMY! WE CAN MAKE A GETAWAY IN THE SEVENMOBILE...!

I'VE LOST HIM! I'LL HAVE TO GET A BETTER VIEW! CHUCKLE...!
ACE BUILDERS LTD.

AHA! THERE HE IS! I'LL NIP ROUND AND PICK HIM UP...!
ZIP
ZOOM

BUT...
HEH, HEH! WANDA WON'T HAVE TIME TO PICK JIMMY UP BEFORE I REACH HIM!
GASP! HE'S RIGHT! BUT POOR OLD JIMMY IS A BAG OF NERVES – AND THAT GIVES ME AN IDEA! CHUCKLE...!
TREMBLE! SHAKE!

YEEK! WHASSAT?
PARP! PARP!
?

HO, HO! A PERFECT LANDING! HOLD TIGHT, JIMMY...!
GASP!
WOW!
BONK!

TEE, HEE! YOU'RE SAFE NOW! WE WERE ONE JUMP AHEAD OF BULLY BRIGGS!
BAH!
ZOOOOOM!

JOKER

HI, MUM! I'VE BROUGHT A FRIEND HOME FOR TEA!
I'VE GOT FRIENDS COMING TOO, JOKER! SO YOU'LL HAVE TO WAIT AND SEE WHAT'S LEFT!

I'LL GO AND GET THE FOOD READY!
BAH! I BET HER FRIENDS WON'T LEAVE ANY GRUB FOR US!

WAIT A MINUTE! I'LL GET OUT MY TRICK CUSHION AND SQUEAKY BUNS..!
HO, HO! WE'LL GET A LAUGH ANYWAY, JOKER!
SQUEAKY BUNS

AND SOON...
COME AND HAVE SOME TEA, LADIES!

EEK! WHASSAT?
GASP! JOKER'S BEEN UP TO HIS TRICKS!
SQUEAK!

YOU TWO CAN LEAVE UNTIL WE'VE FINISHED OUR TEA!
ER...YES, MUM!

DO HAVE A NICE BUN, LADIES!
SQUEAKY BUNS

SQUEAK!
SQUEAK!
ER... NO THANK YOU!
WE'RE NOT FEELING HUNGRY!

UM...I THINK WE'D BETTER BE GOING NOW! GOODBYE!
OH, DEAR! SORRY YOU HAVE TO LEAVE SO SOON! I'LL SEE YOU OUT!

BAH! THEY MUST'VE SPOTTED THE BOX, JOKER! YOUR TRICK DIDN'T WORK!
CHUCKLE! YES IT DID..! THAT WAS THE IDEA..!
SQUEAKY BUNS

THEY'RE REAL BUNS ON THE PLATE! I LEFT THE TRICK ONES IN THE BOX! TUCK IN! CHUCKLE!
HO, HO! YOU REALLY TAKE THE CAKE, JOKER!
SQUEAKY BUNS

The HAUNTED WOOD

I'LL TAKE IT BY SURPRISE AND GET BACK BEFORE IT GETS THE CHANCE TO DO ANYTHING ELSE!
HEH, HEH! THAT'S FOOLED IT! IT'S NOT DOING A THING TO STOP ME!
BEND!
CURL!
G-GASP! HOW DID THAT HAPPEN?
ROLL!
WHERE ARE YOU GOING, HENRY? YOUR DINNER'S READY!
HELP! PUT ME DOWN!
ROLL!
TREAD!
RUMBLE!
OH, NO! N-NOT HERE...!
GLOOP!
SPLOOSH!
SPLOOSH!
HO, HO! I KNEW THAT MAN'S BRIDGE WOULD BE BACK! HE WON'T GET OVER THAT IN A HURRY! CHUCKLE!

My Bruvver

DO I HAVE TO TAKE LITTL'UN TO THE CHRISTMAS PARTY, MUM?
OF COURSE YOU DO, LEN!

AND SOON...
THANKS FOR THE PRESENT, LEN!
YIPPEE! ME SEE FOOD...!

GRR! NOBODY TOLD YOU TO TAKE THAT PIE, LITTL'UN! LET ME HAVE IT!
TEE, HEE! OKAY!

HERE YOU ARE! CHUCKLE!
YIKES!
GLOOP!

S-SORRY ABOUT THAT! PERHAPS WE COULD HAVE A GAME TO KEEP LITTL'UN QUIET!
BAH! VERY WELL! WE'LL PLAY MUSICAL CHAIRS...!

AND, EVENTUALLY...
IT'S JUST YOU AND I LEFT, LITTL'UN! AND NO CHEATING!
CHUCKLE! OKAY, LEN!

THE MUSIC'S STOPPED, LITTL'UN! I'VE WON!
CHUCKLE! THAT'S WHAT LEN THINKS...!

YEEARRGH! HOLLY!
GASP! MY PRESENTS!

BAH! I'D BETTER OPEN THEM NOW TO SEE IF THEY'RE ALL RIGHT!
TEE, HEE! ME HELP MYSELF TO A PRIZE FOR WINNING THE MUSICAL CHAIRS...!

BAH! ME ONLY GOT A WEENY BOX OF CHOCOLATES!
GRR! HE'S UNWRAPPED THE PRIZE FOR OUR PASS THE PARCEL GAME!
CHOCS

DON'T WORRY! WE'LL STILL HAVE OUR GAME—AND MAKE LITTL'UN "WRAP UP" AT THE SAME TIME!
HELP!
CHOCS

TEE, HEE! FIRST ONE TO UNWRAP LITTL'UN WHEN THE MUSIC STOPS WINS THE CHOCOLATES!
HO, HO! I BET LITTL'UN FEELS A "PRIZE" TWIT! CHUCKLE!
SHRIEK! PUT ME DOWN!

MOOSE

SURPRISE, SURPRISE! YOU WON'T BE ABLE TO OUT-RUN ME ZIS TIME, MOOSE!

HEE, HEE! THERE'S NO FOREST FOR YOU TO HIDE IN, EITHER!

ZIS HELICOPTER WILL FOLLOW YOU ANYWHERE YOU RUN TO!

ZUT! I AM CAUGHT ON ZE BRANCH AND I AM UP ZE WRONG WAY!

HELP! I AM FLYING DOWNWARDS AND SCREWING MYSELF INTO ZE GROUND!
CRASH!

DO THAT, IT'S SAFER FOR YOU! HA, HA!
NEXT TIME, MOOSE — I HUNT YOU ON ZE FEET!

JOKER'S JOKES
STICK'EM UP, AND NO FUNNY BUSINESS!
YOU'LL NEVER GET ME UP IN ONE OF THOSE THINGS!
RESTAURANT
HAVE YOU A RESERVATION, SIR?
DO YOU THINK WE SHOULD FEED THE FISH MORE OFTEN?
FISH FOOD

SON of SIR

TEE, HEE! IT'S FUN DURING THE HOLIDAYS! WE DON'T HAVE TO PUT UP WITH SON AND SIR!

BUT...
WRONG, BOYS! TAKE THAT!
ARRGH! GLUB! IT'S THEM!
GRR! WE'LL GET THEM BACK!

YOU WON'T GET THE CHANCE, BOYS! WE'RE OFF! SNIGGER!
GASP! THEY'RE ON SKIS! AFTER THEM ON THE SLEDGES, LADS..!
ZIP!
ZIP!

HUR, HUR! YOU CAN'T STEER SLEDGES LIKE SKIS! SO LONG, BOYS!
SWERVE!
OH, NO! LOOK OUT!

YEEARRGH!
CRASH!
WHAT THE..? GRR! MY FENCE!
SPLINTER!

GRR! COME WITH ME, YOU HOOLIGANS!
CHUCKLE! THE BOYS WILL BE FOR IT NOW, SON! SEE WHAT HE DOES TO THEM..!

WE'RE CLEARING... OFF... INSTEAD..!
GASP! I'LL GET DAD TO STOP THEM..!

GRR! DON'T WORRY, SON! WE'LL GET THE OWNER TO HELP US LOOK FOR THEM..!
ZIP!
ZIP!
GOOD IDEA, DAD!

ARRGH! THE SNOW'S GONE!
HELP!
ZOOM!
TIP!
SCRAPE!

OUCH!
BONK!
CLUNK!
HO, HO! WE SAID, "WE'RE CLEARING THE SNOW OFF THE PATH INSTEAD OF GETTING A WHACKING"!

GRR! THERE'S MORE SNOW THAN EVER, THANKS TO YOU TWO!
SPLOOSH!
OOER..!

HO, HO! SON REALLY LED SIR UP THE GARDEN PATH THIS TIME!
BAH!

FUSS POT
WE'RE NEARLY READY FOR YOUR CHRISTMAS PARTY, FUSS POT!
BAH! THIS ROOM'S TOO SMALL TO HAVE A PARTY!

FOLLOW ME! I'M FUSSY ABOUT WHERE I HAVE MY PARTIES...!
OH, DEAR! WHERE'S FUSS POT TAKING US NOW?

YOU'LL HAVE TO CANCEL THAT! I WANT TO HIRE THE TOWN HALL FOR MY PARTY! FUSS! FUSS!
MAYOR'S BANQUET TODAY
OOER...I DAREN'T ARGUE WITH FUSS POT!

GASP! THIS IS COSTING ME A FORTUNE, FUSS POT!
STOP FUSSING! I'VE GOT TO SEE MY GUESTS ARRIVING..!

FUSS POT'S PARTY— EVERYONE WELCOME
WOW! LET'S GO IN..!

OH NO YOU DON'T! YOU TWO ARE FAR TOO SCRUFFY TO COME TO MY PARTY! FUSS!
FUSS POT'S PARTY- EVERYONE WELCOME WHO COMES UP TO MY VERY FUSSY STANDARDS

MUCH FUSSING LATER...
H'MM... YOU'RE THE ONLY ONE WHO PASSES THE TEST! IN YOU COME!
BOO! THAT'S NOT FAIR!

BAH! D'YOU MEAN I'VE PAID ALL THIS JUST FOR ONE PERSON?
DON'T WORRY, MR. POT! I'VE AN IDEA..!
BILL

LET'S START THE PARTY WITH A GAME OF BLIND MAN'S BUFF, FUSS POT!
VERY WELL! I'LL BE FIRST! FUSS!

TITTER! OOPS... IT SLIPPED, FUSS POT!
WHAT ARE YOU DOING..? GASP!

COME IN, KIDS! FUSS POT HASN'T GOT MUCH SAY IN THE MATTER, NOW! CHUCKLE!
MMM... FUSS, FUSS!

BONEY

OOER! HIDE, BONEY... IT'S YOUR NASTY OWNER WHO WANTS TO TAKE YOU BACK TO THE GHOST TRAIN!

AHA! SO THAT'S WHERE THE BAG OF BONES IS HIDING!
RATTLE! RATTLE!

GOTCHA... ERK!
RATTLE

HOW DARE YOU TRY AND PINCH MY BABY'S RATTLE! TAKE THAT!
ZAP!
YEEEOW!

THAT SOUNDS LIKE BONEY ALL RIGHT! I'VE GOT HIM THIS TIME!
RATTLE! RATTLE!

BACK TO THE GHOST TRAIN, BONEY... HEY!
THWUMP!
LUDO

GRR! I'LL TEACH YOU TO INTERRUPT OUR GAME OF LUDO!
AAGH! IT WAS THE DICE I HEARD!

WE'LL HIDE IN THE ZOO, BONEY!
ZOO

I CAN HEAR RATTLING FROM THE BAG OF BONES! I CAN'T BE MISTAKEN THIS TIME!
REPTILE HOUSE
RATTLE! RATTLE!

REPTILE HOUSE
I'VE GOT HIM CORNERED! I'LL LEAP ON HIM AND GRAB HIM!
RATTLE! RATTLE!

EEEEK! NO—A RATTLE-SNAKE!
RATTLE!

REPTILE HOUSE
BONEY RATTLING WITH LAUGHTER!
RATTLE RATTLE
I'M GETTING OUT OF HERE! I CAN HEAR SOMETHING RATTLING BEHIND THAT ELEPHANT, BUT IT CAN'T BE BONEY... I BET IT'S SOMETHING ELSE THAT'S HORRIBLE!

SAMMY SHRINK

The smallest boy in the world!

HELP! I DIDN'T MEAN TO CLOBBER YOU!
AND I DON'T MEAN TO CLOBBER YOU — I'M GOING TO PULVERISE YOU!
P'RAPS HE'LL LEAVE ME ALONE NOW!

BAH! I'VE LOST HIM!
SKID!

LATER ...
SNOWMAN CONTEST TO DAY!
BUILD SNOWMEN HERE!
I HOPE MINE'S BIG ENOUGH TO WIN A PRIZE!

HELP! THE BRANCH HAS BROKEN!
SO THAT'S WHERE THAT BIG BULLY WAS HIDING!!!

RIGHT, SHRINK— NOW YOU'RE FOR IT! EEK!!
PLOP!

WHAT A MARVELLOUS SNOWMAN! YOU WIN FIRST PRIZE!
COO, TA!
JUDGE
WINTER HUMBUGS GIANT SIZE!

IF WE ALL BREATHE HARD ON HIM, P'RAPS HE'LL THAW OUT!
NOT BEFORE WE'VE FINISHED THESE—I HOPE! SLURP!
THAT SPELL IN THE COOLER WILL TEACH HIM A LESSON!
HUMBUGS

BEAT YOUR NEIGHBOUR

COO! TARZAN WAS GREAT!
THIS WEEK—
TARZAN
HUH! BET MY DAD COULD DO ANYTHING HE DID!

SO...
HEE, HEE! MY DAD'S TARZAN COSTUME IS BETTER THAN THAT THREAD-BARE RUG YOUR DAD'S GOT!
GRR!

GRR! BET I CAN DO TARZAN'S JUNGLE CALL BETTER THAN YOU!
NO, YOU CAN'T— AND I'LL PROVE IT!

HO, HO! YOUR DAD'S COSTUME WAS FULL OF MOTHS!
WAAOOAAOOAH!
WAAOOOAAAOHH!
YAH! MORE MOTHS CAME OUT OF YOUR DAD'S!

GRRR! LOOK WHAT THOSE MOTHS ARE DOING! SCRAG 'EM, GIRLS!
HEEELP!

FARTHER ON...
BET MY DAD CAN TALK TO ANIMALS, JUST LIKE TARZAN!
MY DAD CAN DO IT BETTER—SHOW 'EM, DAD!

?
MOOOOOo!
BELLOW!
WOW!

GRRR! MAKE A FOOL OF MY VOICE, EH?
QUICK! OVER THIS FENCE!
RUMBLE!
YERK! THEY WERE TOO GOOD!

NO TRESPASSING PENALTY £20
OY! CAN'T YOU LOT READ?
OH, NO!
OOER! WE'VE JUMPED INTO AN ARMY ASSAULT COURSE!

PAY UP!
I THINK WE'D BETTER GET OUT OF HERE!
GRRR!

SNARL! WAIT TILL WE CATCH YOU!
OOER! MY DAD'S JUST LIKE TARZAN, SWINGING THROUGH THE JUNGLE CREEPERS!
ERK! SO'S MINE—AND HE'S CATCHING UP!

THE GROUP
BRAIN
LUVVY
FATSO
STUPID
SHORTY
RINGO

LARDER
IT'S MY TURN TO GUARD THE GRUB. YOU NEED TO GUARD IT WHEN YOU'VE GOT A GLUTTEN LIKE FATSO IN YOUR GANG!

HERE HE COMES NOW!
GASP! GASP! GASP!

GASP! GASP! GOT TO HAVE FOOD! FOOD!
HE CERTAINLY PUTS ON A GOOD ACT!
CLAW!

HOP IT, YOU GREEDY PIG! WE HAD DINNER ONLY TEN MINUTES AGO!
AAGH! ROTTER!

HEH, HEH! THIS ELEPHANT COSTUME WILL FOOL HIM!

COO! WHERE DID JUMBO COME FROM? LUVVY MUST BE GOING IN FOR KING-SIZE PETS!
?

HELP! A TRUNK WITH A TONGUE!!!??
DROOL! DROOL!

AAGHEE!
I SHOULD HAVE KNOWN IT! ONLY FATSO COULD HAVE A TONGUE THAT LONG!
LEAP!
STAB!

GRRR! ONLY ONE THING FOR IT – I'LL HAVE TO GET SHOT OF OLD SHORTY BY FORCE!

COO! WHAT YOU GOING TO DO WITH THAT, FATSO?
ER – NOTHING, LUVVY! YOU KNOW I NEVER USE VIOLENCE – I'M A LAD OF PEACE!

GOOD - I'LL PUT IT ON THE FIRE THEN I WON'T HAVE TO GO OUT FOR WOOD!
SHE'S CLOBBERED ME CLUB! NOW I'LL HAVE TO THINK OF SOMETHING ELSE!

HEH, HEH! I'LL KNOCK OUT SHORTY WITH THIS SLEEPING GAS I MADE FROM STALE CHEESE AND OLD SOCKS!
FATSO'S K.O. SPRA

AAH! GOOD OLD FATSO! YOU'VE BOUGHT A NEW AIR FRESHENER!
SNATCH!
?
NO, BRAIN! YOU'VE GOT IT ALL WRONG!

DEADLY PONG!
AAH... DELICIOUS... ER... I THINK!

PONG!
URG!
PHEW!
THUMP!

EVERYONE'S SPOILING EVERYTHING! HE'S SPRAYED OUT THE LAST DROP!
TWEET!
TWEET!

NOT TO WORRY! I'LL JUST LASSO HIM!

BUT SOMETHING GOES WRONG...
?
SPIN!
WHIRL!
WHIRL!
WHEEEEE!

AAGH! HELP! GET ME OUT, SOMEBODY!
FATSO'S WRAPPED UP IN SOME ROPEY STUNT!
LOOKS CRAZY TO ME - AND I'M STUPID!

COO! HE'S FALLEN THRO' OUR SECRET EXIT TRAP DOOR!
CRASH!

GOSH! WHAT A MESS! GET THE DOCTOR, STUPID!

LATER...
TEA UP! NOSH FOR YOUR GNASHERS!

HO, HO! POOR OLD FATSO CAN'T JOIN US!
MAYBE HE'LL WAIT NEXT TIME!
BOO-HOO! THAT ROTTEN DOC DIDN'T EVEN LEAVE A HOLE FOR MY MOUTH! SOB! SOB!
DELICIOUS, LUVVY! CHOMP! CHOMP!
BUMPER ICE CREAM
DOCTOR
I'LL PRESCRIBE FATSO'S PORTION - FOR ME!

THUNDERBALL
of the
SUPER SEVEN

RIGHT! LET'S SEE YOU SAVE THIS ONE! CHUCKLE!
YIKES! TAKE IT EASY, THUNDERBALL!

OOPS!
KICK!
GASP! ARE YOU TRYING TO TAKE OVER BOOTER'S JOB?

DON'T WORRY, LADS! I'LL GO IN AND GET OUR BALL BACK..!

BUT...
HAW, HAW! HERE'S ANOTHER TARGET FOR ME TO PRACTICE ON..!
YIKES! HE MEANS OUR BALL! I'D BETTER DO SOMETHING..!
MARVO THE FANTASTIC KNIFE THROWER

THAT'S SHIFTED IT! LET'S GRAB OUR BALL AND RUN, LADS!
ZIP!
BONK!
GASP! THAT MUST'VE BEEN A LUCKY SHOT!

GOT IT! NOW WE CAN GO!
HEH, HEH! THAT'S WHAT THEY THINK..!

I'M NOT HAVING BALLS KICKED INTO MY GARDEN, SO YOU CAN HAND IT OVER! SNIGGER!
MARVO
H'MM... IT'S TIME I SHOWED HIM ONE OF MY TRICKS!
MARVO
CRACK
ZING!
NOW FOR SOME QUICK-FIRE SHOTS TO HELP US GET AWAY!
MARBLES

SPLINTER!
ARRGH! WHAT ARE YOU DOING? STOPPIT!
TEE, HEE! ANY MINUTE NOW...!
CRACK!
WHEEEEEEEEEEEEEEEEEEEEEEEEEE
ZINNNNNNNNNNNG!
ZIPPPPPPPPPPPPPPPPPPPPPPP
FLIP!
FLIP!
FLIP!
MARBLES

SPLINTER!
EEK! I'M FALLING THROUGH!
CHUCKLE! OUT WE GO, LADS..!

HO, HO! THANKS, THUNDERBALL! YOU REALLY HELPED US OUT OF A HOLE! CHUCKLE!
BAH! GROAN!
MARVO

MOOSE

FRENCHY'S COMING! WHERE CAN I HIDE?
GULP! I CAN'T THINK, MOOSE!

FRENCHY'S COMING! WHERE CAN I HIDE?
DUH... NO IDEA, MOOSE!

HEH! MOOSE 'AS GIVEN HIMSELF AWAY ZIS TIME!

I'LL AIM STRAIGHT THROUGH ZE BUSH!
PROD!

WATCH WHO YOU'RE PRODDING, MATE! GRRR!
I DON'T NEED TO ASK BRUIN WHERE I SHOULD HIDE NOW!
BLAM!

BAFFLING BALLOONS

Pete's balloon has got mixed up with two from his pockets. Which one is he holding?

Answer: A

Cooky

PLAY SCHOOL
I'M GOING TO LOOK AFTER THESE CHILDREN WHILE THEIR MUMMIES ARE SHOPPING!

THAT BOX OF TOYS WILL KEEP YOU ALL OCCUPIED, KIDS!
TOYS
COR!

WHAT TOYS? A RING GAME WITH NO RINGS!
A DRAUGHT BOARD WITH NO DRAUGHTS!
AND A FEW BUILDING BRICKS!

WE WANT SOME TOYS!
WE WANT TOYS!
QUIET, CHILDREN... PLEASE! OH, DEAR... WHAT SHALL I DO TO KEEP THEM OCCUPIED?

I KNOW... I'LL COOK THEM SOME TASTY SNACKS!
WE WANT TOYS!

DOUGHNUTS... BISCUITS... ROCK CAKES! YES, THAT SHOULD KEEP THEM QUIET!
COOKERY
HERE YOU ARE, CHILDREN! I'VE MADE YOU SOME SCRUMMY SNACKS!
BAH! WE WANT TOYS— NOT FOOD!

HOWEVER, A LITTLE LATER...
UTTER SILENCE
THE KIDS ARE QUIET... MY COOKING MUST HAVE WORKED THE TRICK! I'LL TAKE A LOOK!

OH, NO... I DON'T BELIEVE IT!

GOOD OL' COOKY... YOUR DOUGHNUTS MAKE SUPER RINGS!
AND IT WAS LUCKY YOU BURNT SOME OF THESE BISCUITS... NOW THEY MAKE IDEAL DRAUGHTS!
AND YOUR ROCK CAKES ARE SO HARD, THEY ARE JUST LIKE BUILDING BRICKS!
OH, WELL... AT LEAST IT'LL KEEP THEM OCCUPIED TILL THEIR MUMS RETURN!

my bruvver

I WANT YOU TO TAKE LITTL'UN TO THE DEPARTMENT STORE TO SEE FATHER CHRISTMAS!
BAH! DO I HAVE TO? HE'S BOUND TO CAUSE TROUBLE!

TO SANTA'S GROTTO
SANTA'S GROTTO
WE'LL HAVE TO QUEUE, LITTL'UN!
I'M NOT WAITING AROUND... I'LL GET RID OF THIS LOT!
TO CARPET DEPT

AND I SEE JUST THE THING I NEED TO DO IT!
HEY...LITTL'UN! COME BACK HERE!

GROWL! ROAR!
RUN FOR YOUR LIVES!
YIKES!
EEK! AN ESCAPED TIGER!
HELP!

GROTTO
LITTL'UN! BAH! I SHOULD HAVE KNOWN!
HEE, HEE! NOW WE'RE FIRST IN THE QUEUE, LEN!

AND WHAT DO YOU WANT FOR CHRISTMAS, LITTLE BOY?
I DON'T KNOW..!
TOYS

HUH?
...I'LL SEE WHAT YOU'VE GOT!
TOYS

OUCH! GET HIM OUTTA THERE! OWCH!
OH, DEAR... MORE TROUBLE!

COME HERE, YOU LITTLE NUISANCE!
BAH! THERE'S NOTHING IN THERE I WANT!

ER... COULD HE HAVE THAT COWBOY OUTFIT, SANTA?
WELL, WE DON'T USUALLY GIVE THOSE TOYS AWAY... BUT ANYTHING TO GET RID OF HIM!
COR!

HEE, HEE! THIS IS JUST THE THING FOR YOU... YOU WON'T CAUSE ANY TROUBLE, NOW!
TOYS
BAH!

The Toffs ...

BAH! IT WASN'T WORTH GOING TO THE FAIR! WE'VE ONLY WON ONE COCONUT BETWEEN US, AND WE'RE F-FREEZING!

YOU CAN HAVE SOME OF OURS, TOUGHS! THANKS TO OUR SUPER HEATING, WE CAN GROW OUR OWN! CHUCKLE!
HEAT!
WAFT!
WOW! IT'S A REAL COCONUT PALM!

CHUCKLE! WE'VE TAKEN ALL WE NEED..!

POING!
...THEY CAN HAVE THE REST! TITTER!
ZOOM!
SPLINTER!
CRASH!
OH, NO! OUR ROOF!

PITY THEY ALL BROKE! STICK AROUND FOR SOME MORE, TOUGHS! DON'T BE "SHY"! CHUCKLE!
TOSS!
YIKES! GRAB A COCONUT SHELL EACH, TOUGHS!

BAH! WE'LL LET THEM MEND THEIR ROOF, THEN SMASH IT AGAIN!
CHUCKLE! WE CAN GET ON WITH OUR JOB, NOW— WE'RE WEARING "CRASH HELMETS"!
BONK!

and the TOUGHS

Beat your Neighbour

YOU WON'T BEAT *THIS!* ***WE*** CAN GET AUSTRALIAN T.V. PROGRAMMES, NOW!
WANT TO BET? WHEN I'VE ADDED THIS EXTRA LENGTH, ***WE'LL*** BE ABLE TO PICK UP T.V. SIGNALS FROM OUTER SPACE!
HI, COBBERS!

OH, NO! THEY'RE STARTING TO BEND!
OOER!
AAAGH!
MY DAD'S MAKING A BETTER DIVE THAN YOUR DAD!
BUT MY DAD'S FALLING FASTER!

KRASH!
KRASH!

MY DAD'S APPEARING ON TELLY—YOURS ISN'T!
BUT MY DAD'S SEEING MORE STARS THAN YOUR DAD!

THE GROUP

BRAIN
LUVVY
FATSO
STUPID
SHORTY
RINGO

IN ANOTHER PART OF TOWN...

L. BAXE
BOOT!
PICK A BETTER HIDING PLACE NEXT TIME!

AJAX BAKERY Co.
THOSE TWERPS ARE USELESS – WATCH AN EXPERT AT WORK!
TIP TOE!

FOOD! FOOD! JUST LOOK AT ALL THAT LOVELY FOOD! SLURP!
SNEAK!

IT PAYS TO HAVE A LONG TONGUE! HEH, HEH!
FLOUR
AAAAGH!

HERE'S SOME YELLOW STUFF TO COAT YOUR TONGUE, MATE!
FLOUR
XXX
FLICK!

AAGH! YOU ROTTEN TWERP! THAT'S MUSTARD! ME TONGUE'S ON FIRE! WAA-AAH!
FAIR EXCHANGE!

AJAX BAKERY Co.
COO! FATSO'S HOLDING HIS TONGUE!
YEAH! BUT HE SHOULD BE HOLDING FLOUR!
AAGH! OOH! OOH! WATER! WATER!

IT LOOKS LIKE IT WILL HAVE TO BE ME AGAIN!

AJAX BAKERY Co.
HEAD
BIG HEAD!
SUPERIOR INTELLIGENCE WILL WIN THROUGH!

I SAY— THEY'VE SPELT FLOUR WRONG THERE! TCH! TCH!
FLOUR

I AIN'T STUPID! THAT'S HOW IT'S SPELT! THAT'S BAKING STUFF IN THERE! NOT GARDEN STUFF! I AIN'T DAFT!

IT JUST SO HAPPENS I HAVE A DICTIONARY WITH ME, DEAR CHAP! I THINK IT WILL PROVE WHO'S RIGHT!

HEH, HEH! I GUESS THIS PROVES I'M RIGHT!
AAAGH! TREACHERY!
LEAP!

YAHOO! I'VE GOT SOME! LET'S GO!
COO! AIN'T BRAIN CLEVER?
FLOUR
XXX

YAHOO! LOVELY DOUGHNUTS! — BRAIN FOR KING!
WHO'S FOR THEIR TWENTY SECOND HELPING?
KEEP THEM COMING UP, LUVVY! SLURP! SLURP!
PIPING HOT
MUNCH!
CHOMP!

BONEY
That's ME, folks!

WE'VE REACHED THE WILDS OF CANADA, BONEY... YOUR OWNER WON'T FIND US HERE!

?
ER... BILLY!
JOIN THE ROYAL CANADIAN MOUNTED POLICE THEY ALWAYS GET THEIR BONES

SHOULDN'T THAT READ 'GET THEIR MAN', BILLY? GULP!
JOIN THE ROYAL CANADIAN MOUNTED POLICE THEY ALWAYS GET THEIR BONES
GASP! YOU'RE RIGHT, BONEY!

WRONG, KID! I'M OUT FOR THE REWARD, TOO, FOR CAPTURING YOU!
AAGH! RUN FOR IT, BONEY!

WHOA, YOU TWO... IT'S NO USE TRYING TO OUTRUN ME!
WAAH!

I WISH THAT MOUNTIE WAS RIDING AN ELEPHANT, BILLY... THEN I COULD SCARE IT WITH MY PET MOUSE! GASP!

CRUMBS! LET'S MAKE A PET OF THE MOOSE, BONEY... IT WOULD SCARE ANYTHING!

G-GULP! I THINK YOU'RE ONLY MAKING THAT BULL-MOOSE SEE RED, BILLY!
N-NICE, MOOSE! P-PRETTY MOOSE!

YIKES! IT IS SEEING RED, BILLY... OUR MOUNTIE CHUM'S RED TUNIC!
YERK!
SNORT!

WAAH! HELP!
ROAR! SNORT!
A MOOSE BEATS A MOUSE EVERY TIME, BILLY!
ESPECIALLY A BULL-MOOSE, BONEY! HO, HO!

SON OF SIR

WE'RE PLAYING RUGBY TODAY, BOYS!
HUH! TRUST SIR'S SON TO BE CAPTAIN!

AW! HE PLAYS TOO ROUGH! I CAN'T GET THE BALL OFF HIM!
SNARL!

ALLOW ME, DEAR BOY!
THANKS, DAD! I MIGHT HAVE HURT MYSELF IF I'D TRIED TO TACKLE HIM FAIRLY!

IF YOU LOT TRY AND TOUCH ME, I'LL GET MY DAD ONTO YOU!
HUH! HE WOULD, TOO!

A BRILLIANT TRY, SON!
BAH!

FOLLOWED BY A MASTERLY CONVERSION!
HEY... THE CROSS-BAR'S MUCH LOWER THAN USUAL! I BET THAT UNFAIR PAIR HAVE BEEN CHEATING AGAIN!
WEEDY KICK!

GRR! SON'S... A ...ROTTEN EGG!
HOW DARE THEY CALL SOMEONE AS NICE AS ME, HORRIBLE NAMES? I'LL SNEAK TO DAD ON THEM!

FOR BEING RUDE ABOUT MY WONDERFUL SON, I'M STOPPING THE GAME! YOU'LL RETURN TO CLASS!
AW!

WE'RE FINISHED, HEADMASTER... CATCH!

SPLODGE!
GHASTLY WHIFF!
GLOOP!

GRR! YOU'LL CATCH IT NOW!
AND SO WILL YOU, SON! YOU STARTED IT ALL, YOU NASTY PIECE OF WORK!
HAW, HAW! WE REALLY SAID..." WE'LL FIX SON'S NONSENSE WITH A HUGE ROTTEN EGG WE FOUND"!

MOOSE
ZUT! I CAN ALMOST SMELL OUT ZE TRAIL OF MOOSE!

HEE, HEE! I'LL HAVE A LITTLE GAME WITH OLD LAFEET!

WHAT THE?
WHIP!

ZUT! ZE PESKY BIRD IS USING MY HAT FOR HIS NEST!

?
GOT IT — EEK— A SKUNK!

HELP! I MUST FIND A RIVER, QUICKLY!
HEE, HEE! SMELLY OLD LAFEET!
WHIFF!
PONG!
SNARL!

THE SUPER SEVEN

FRAME-UP

At first glance these two pictures from a Super Seven story appear to be identical – but the bottom one has been „got at". The artist has made 10 crafty alterations . . . see if you can spot them. (Answers below).

Whistler's straw bends the wrong way, crease lines longer on Santa's sack, Christmas tree branch longer, no cherry on kid's cake, longer garland, Dead Eye Dick's glass empty, kid wearing long trousers, extra bauble on Christmas tree, thicker white stripes on Booter's jersey, no colour on kid's shirt.

STINKER
of the
SUPER SEVEN

SCHOOL
WOW! WHAT'S THAT LOVELY SMELL? IT CAN'T BE ONE OF YOUR STINK BOMBS, STINKER!

FISH AND CHIP SHOP
WHIRR!
WAFT!
OPEN
COO! IT'S A NEW FISH AND CHIP SHOP! LET'S BUY SOME!
BAH! HOW CAN WE? WE'RE ALL BROKE!

WHY DON'T WE SING A FEW CAROLS AS IT'S NEARLY CHRISTMAS?
OPEN
GOOD IDEA, STINKER! WE'LL PUT OUR CAPS ON THE GROUND TO COLLECT THE CASH! CHUCKLE!

GOOD KING WENCESLAS LOOKED OUT...
BAH! I'M NOT HAVING THAT ROW OUTSIDE MY POSH NEW SHOP...!
TAKE THAT!
ARRGH! LUCKY HE'S A ROTTEN SHOT!
SPLOOSH!

NOW, CLEAR OFF FROM MY SHOP!
BAH! I SUPPOSE WE'LL HAVE TO, LADS! PICK UP YOUR CAPS..!

HAW, HAW! I DIDN'T MISS YOUR CAPS! NOW CLEAR OFF BEFORE I MAKE A STINK!
GRR! HE WANTS A **STINK**, DOES HE..?
SPLOOSH!
SPLOSH!

LET'S SEE HOW HE LIKES ONE OF **MY** STINK BOMBS..!
SNIGGER!
BUT YOU'LL NEVER GET IT THROUGH WITH THAT FAN TURNING, STINKER!

CLANK!
GRIND!
CRUNCH
TEE, HEE! IT'S NOT MEANT TO GO **THROUGH**!
OPEN

GASP! WE'RE NOT GOING THERE! WE LIKE **FRESH** FISH!
WAFT!
PONG!
PHEW!
OPEN
YIKES!

SOB! COME IN AND HAVE A FREE MEAL, KIDS! JUST TO PROVE MY FISH IS FRESH!
OPEN
OKAY, MISTER! IF YOU INSIST! CHUCKLE!

AND SO...
KEEP 'EM COMING, MISTER! THEY'RE STILL NOT CONVINCED! CHUCKLE!
TEE, HEE! WHAT A LAUGH— THIS LOT WOULD HAVE COST US A **BOMB**! TITTER!
CLICK!
GROAN!

Sammy Shrink

SAMMY! ARE YOU SURE YOU CAN CARRY THAT BAR OF TOFFEE?
SWEET SHOP
YUM, YUM! NOT HALF!

CHEEK! I'M AS STRONG AS ANY BOY!
THIS WAY HOME
BEAN

SAMMY! I HOPE YOU HAVEN'T BEEN BUYING MORE TOFFEE!
OO-ER! I'D BETTER HIDE IT!

DAD WARNED YOU THAT HE'S STOPPING YOUR SWEETS!
COO! SO HE DID!

I'LL HIDE THE TOFFEE UP HERE! OOO — IT'S MELTING!

HELP! I'M STUCK ON THE CUCKOO!

ERK! I CAN HEAR DAD — HE'S HOME! I-I'D BETTER STICK WHERE I AM!

CLICK!
CLICK!
WHERE'S SAMMY? NOT OUT BUYING MORE SWEETS, I HOPE!
GOSH! DAD SOUNDS ANGRY!

CLICK!
CUCKOO! CUCKOO!
HELP! THE CLOCK'S STRUCK!

URK!
SPLUTT!
WOOSH!
BOING!
SPLASH!
BOING!
NOW I'M RIGHT IN THE SOUP!

UG-GLUGG!
DAD'S EATING MY TOFFEE...!

I'LL BUY SHERBET NEXT TIME, DAD! NO MORE TOFFEE — I PROMISE!
GRRRRRRRRRR!

The FULL HOUSE

THE FAMILY ARE GETTING READY FOR NEXT SUMMER'S HOLIDAY IN THEIR NEW CARAVAN! THEY'RE SLEEPING IN IT TONIGHT TO GET USED TO IT!

THANKS FOR LOOKING AFTER OUR PETS, MRS SCROOGE! IT'LL BE GOOD PRACTISE FOR WHEN WE REALLY DO GO AWAY!

BAH! SHE'S TOO MEAN TO GIVE US ENOUGH GRUB — I'LL STOW AWAY..!

GASP! I CAN'T PULL THE LINE! THOSE PULLEYS MUST HAVE RUSTED UP!
WE'LL GET SOME OIL, MUM..!

STAND ASIDE! THIS JOB CALLS FOR A STRONG MAN!

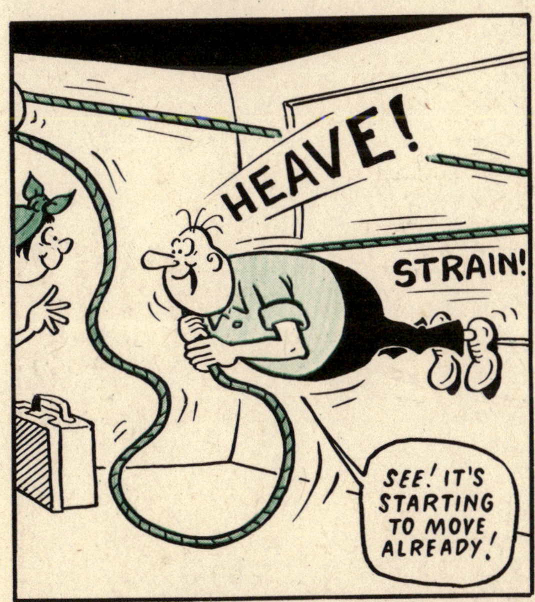
HEAVE!
STRAIN!
SEE! IT'S STARTING TO MOVE ALREADY!

OH, NO! S-STOP PULLING, DAD!
EEK! WE'RE MOVING!
TUG!
PULL!
TRUNDLE!

CRUNCH!
TEE, HEE! THEY WON'T BE GOING FAR IN THAT!
YIKES! TOO LATE!

BAH! I'LL HAVE TO SPEND OUR HOLIDAY MONEY ON REPAIRING OUR CARAVAN! WE'LL HAVE TO STAY HERE!
YIPPEE! BACK TO FULL RATIONS—WE WOULDN'T FEEL AT HOME ANYWHERE ELSE!

Pete's POCKETS

YIPPEE! GOOD OLD JACK...HE'S TURNED THE RAIN INTO SNOW!
A PLEASURE!
HEE, HEE! OUR SNOWMAN WILL BE SAFE UNTIL TOMORROW!
YIPPEE! SEE YOU THEN, PETE!
BUT, NEXT MORNING...
OOH! I SEE IT'S STILL JUST RIGHT FOR SNOWMEN!
ARRGH! I'VE BLUNDERED! IT SNOWED SO MUCH THAT OUR SNOWMAN'S BURIED!
GRR! SO YOU'RE BEHIND THIS, PETE! COME DOWN AND GET THIS PATH CLEARED AT ONCE!

The HAUNTED WOOD
DON'T TAKE THAT WOOD AWAY, MISTER! IT'S HAUNTED!
PAH! DON'T TALK NONSENSE, LAD! I NEED IT FOR A BATTERING-RAM!
AND...
HEH, HEH! PAY UP THE MONEY YOU OWE ME, OR I'LL BASH THE DOOR DOWN!
OOER...BUT I CAN'T AFFORD IT TILL NEXT WEEK!
RIGHT! YOU ASKED FOR IT! HERE I COME...!
THUNDER!
ARRGH! WHAT'S HAPPENED? STRAIGHTEN UP, YOU STUPID TRUNK!
BEND!
DIG!
AND IT DID...!
YEEARRGH!
POING!
CRUNCH!
HO, HO! YOU WON'T BREAK MY DOOR DOWN LIKE THAT!
GNN!
ZOOM!

GRR! I DON'T KNOW WHAT WENT WRONG, BUT I'LL TRY AGAIN...!
BUT...
YIKES! IT'S TAKEN ROOT!
EEEK! THE TRUNK'S COMING ALIVE! IT'S GROWN SOME HORNS!
HELP! IT'S TURNED INTO A REAL RAM!
HO, HO! AND NOW IT'S BATTERING HIM! CHUCKLE!
YEEOUCH!
BIFF!
SHRIEK! K-KEEP IT OFF! HE CAN KEEP HIS ROTTEN MONEY!
TEE, HEE! I KNEW ALL HE'D "GET INTO" WAS TROUBLE WITH THAT HAUNTED WOOD! CHUCKLE!

SON of SIR

GOOD MORNING, BOYS! PUT THOSE SNOWBALLS DOWN AT ONCE!
WHY, SIR? IN CASE WE BREAK A WINDOW?

NO, SO THAT MY SON CAN GET A FREE POT-SHOT AT YOU ALL! SNIGGER!
THANKS, DAD! CHORTLE!
GLUB!
SPLAT!

MUMBLE! MUTTER!
TEE, HEE! NO DOUBT THEY'RE PLOTTING REVENGE! FIND OUT WHAT THEY'RE UP TO, SON!

WAIT 'TILL SON AND SIR REACH... DOOR... SLIPPERY... FALL DOWN! SNIGGER!

THERE'S A SLIPPERY BIT BY THE DOOR, DAD! THEY THINK WE'LL FALL DOWN!
IS THAT SO?
DIG!

WELL, THIS WILL PUT PAID TO THEIR LITTLE GAME!
SCATTER!
?
?
?
?

TEE, HEE! WE'VE MADE IT WITHOUT SKIDDING—SPOILED THEIR FUN!
ERK! L-LOOK OUT!

ERK!
YEEAAAGH!
SHRIEK! MY NEWLY-POLISHED FLOOR!
SLIP!
SKID!

OOOOF! WHAT THE..?
UGGGH! H-HEADMASTER!
WHUMP!
GNNN!

SO...
GRR ... CLUMSY CLOTS! YOU CAN POLISH THE FLOOR AGAIN FOR THIS POOR WOMAN!
HEH, HEH! ALL I SAID WAS "WAIT 'TILL SON AND SIR REACH THE DOOR, IT'S SLIPPERY INSIDE AND THEY'LL FALL DOWN"!

YAAH! WE CAN GET OUR OWN BACK NOW!
EEK! HELP, DAD! MY ARMS ARE TOO TIRED TO THROW SNOWBALLS!
GROAN! MY ARMS ARE TOO TIRED TO DO ANY CANING!
THROB!

WHISTLER of the SUPER SEVEN

AND SOON...
THERE HE IS! I'LL TRY ANOTHER WHISTLE!
B-BUT HE'LL HEAR IT AGAIN, WHISTLER!

SILENCE!
EH..? WHISTLER'S LOST HIS TOUCH!
!

BAH! THAT WAS NO USE! NOBODY COULD HEAR THAT!
TEE, HEE! MAYBE NOT..!

WOOF
GURR!
OH, NO- POLICE DOGS!
...BUT THEY DID! CHUCKLE!
GROWL!
WOOF!

SNAP!
GRR!
SNARL!
RRIP
ARRGH! K-KEEP 'EM OFF! I GIVE UP!
GNASH!
HO, HO! WELL DONE, WHISTLER! THOSE DOGS MUST THINK HE'S A "CAT" BURGLAR! CHUCKLE!

MOOSE

HIYA, CHIEF!

ZUT! INDIAN CHIEF DOESN'T WEAR ZE TAIL. EET MUST BE ZE MOOSE!

YOU CANNOT FOOL ME, MOOSE!
GULP! MY INDIAN TRICK DIDN'T WORK!
INDIAN RESERVATION-UGH!

AHA! MOOSE CAN'T FOOL LAFEET AGAIN WITH ZAT ZILLY INDIAN DISGUISE!

ZIS TIME I DON'T MINCE ZE WORDS, I MINCE YOU INSTEAD, LIKE ZO...
BOP!
UGH!

STOPPUM STILL WHILE I SCALPUM YOU!

The SUPER 7
SUPER 7

YOU'VE GOT TO HELP, SUPER SEVEN! SOMEONE'S PINCHING ALL THE TOYS FROM MY STORE!
HMM... WE'D BETTER TAKE A LOOK AROUND..!
Clamidges
SUPER 7

HEY! IT'S NOT CHRISTMAS FOR A WEEK, YET! SANTA'S A BIT EARLY!
I'D BETTER CHECK!

BAH! LOOK AT THAT! IT'S A BURGLAR IN DISGUISE!
YIKES! THEY'VE GOT "WIND" OF MY PLAN!

I'LL RAISE THE ALARM WHILE YOU BRING HIM DOWN, THUNDERBALL!
OKAY, DEAD EYE..!

YEEARRGH!

YIKES! HE'S NOT EVEN SHAKEN!
HEH, HEH! THAT'S RIGHT..!

HAW, HAW! MY SANTA DISGUISE "CUSHIONED" MY FALL!
GASP! HE'S ONLY A SKINNY BLOKE!

SO LONG, SUCKERS!
GRR! HE'S BOUND TO STRIKE AGAIN! WE'LL SET A TRAP FOR HIM..!

AND SO...
CHUCKLE! THIS EMPTY TOY SACK THE STORE MANAGER GAVE US WILL DO THE TRICK!
TEE, HEE! IT WILL WITH A FEW OF MY STINK BOMBS IN IT! GET READY TO CLOSE IT, WINDY..!
STINK BOMBS

DONE IT!
SUPER 7
SWELL!
HO, HO! THAT'S TRAPPED THE STINK INSIDE! COME ON—WE'D BETTER HIDE! CHUCKLE...!

AND SOON...
lamidgos
WOW! SOMEONE'S LEFT A SACK OF TOYS! WHAT EASY PICKINGS!
CHUCKLE! THAT'S WHAT HE THINKS...!

HEH, HEH! I'LL TAKE THIS BACK TO MY HIDE-OUT...!
CHUCKLE! NOW WE'LL FIND OUT WHERE HE'S KEEPING ALL THE KIDS' TOYS...

HEH! I'LL OPEN THE SACK INSIDE..!
HO, HO! HE WON'T BE INSIDE FOR LONG! DO YOUR STUFF, BOOTER..!

HOW'S THAT? CHUCKLE!
KICK!
PLOP!
PONG!
WHAT THE... ARRGH!

UGH! LEMME OUT! IT'S 'ORRIBLE!
I'LL GET AFTER HIM! BE READY WITH THE LASSO, DEAD EYE!

I'LL JUST GET MY AIM RIGHT..!
GRR! THIS'LL FIX THAT KID..!

TAKE THAT! SNIGGER!
ARGH! GLUB!

YERK! I'M FROZEN SOLID!
GRR! IF DEAD EYE CAN'T SWING THE LASSO, I WILL! LUCKY THE CROOK MADE THAT PATCH OF ICE..!
SUPER 7

CHUCKLE! LET GO, DEAD EYE!
WHAT THE..? YIKES!

TEE, HEE! GOT HIM!
YERK!

HEY! WH-WHAT ABOUT ME? I'M F-FREEZING!
HO, HO! WHISTLER WILL SORT YOU OUT WHILE WE PICK UP ALL THE STOLEN TOYS..!

WOW! THANKS, WHISTLER! LET'S GET THOSE TOYS BACK TO THE STORE..!
PHEEP!

AND SO...
THANKS, SUPER SEVEN! THE KIDS WILL HAVE SOMETHING TO SPEND THEIR CHRISTMAS MONEY ON, NOW!
SUPER 7
TEE, HEE! I KNOW WHERE THIS CROOK WILL BE 'SPENDING' HIS CHRISTMAS! HAVE A SUPER TIME, EVERY-ONE! CHUCKLE!

KANGAROO KID

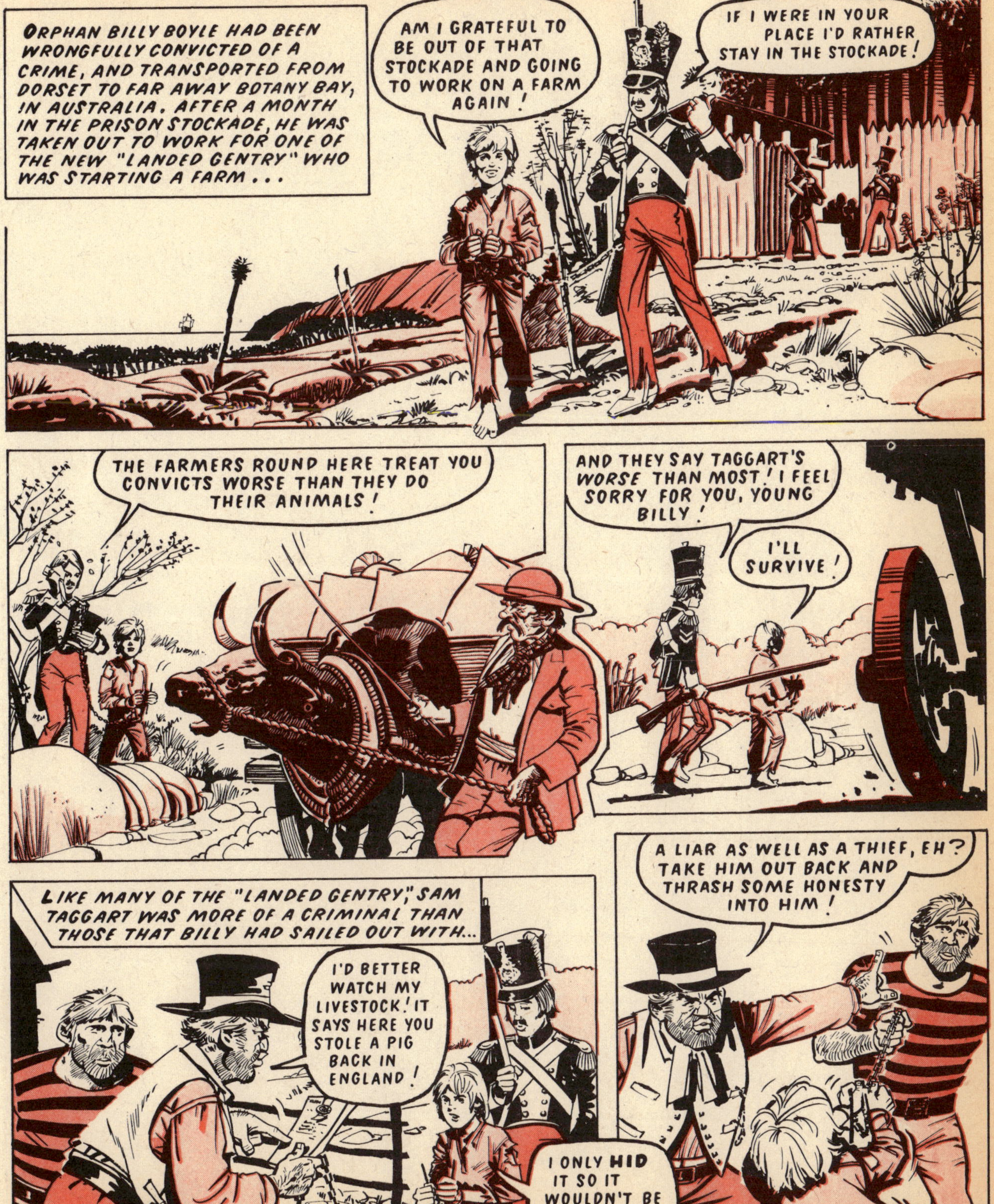

THE FARMERS ROUND HERE TREAT YOU CONVICTS WORSE THAN THEY DO THEIR ANIMALS!

AND THEY SAY TAGGART'S *WORSE* THAN MOST! I FEEL SORRY FOR YOU, YOUNG BILLY!

I'LL SURVIVE!

LIKE MANY OF THE "LANDED GENTRY," SAM TAGGART WAS MORE OF A CRIMINAL THAN THOSE THAT BILLY HAD SAILED OUT WITH...

I'D BETTER WATCH MY LIVESTOCK! IT SAYS HERE YOU STOLE A PIG BACK IN ENGLAND!

I ONLY **HID** IT SO IT WOULDN'T BE SENT TO THE SLAUGHTER-HOUSE!

A LIAR AS WELL AS A THIEF, EH? TAKE HIM OUT BACK AND THRASH SOME HONESTY INTO HIM!

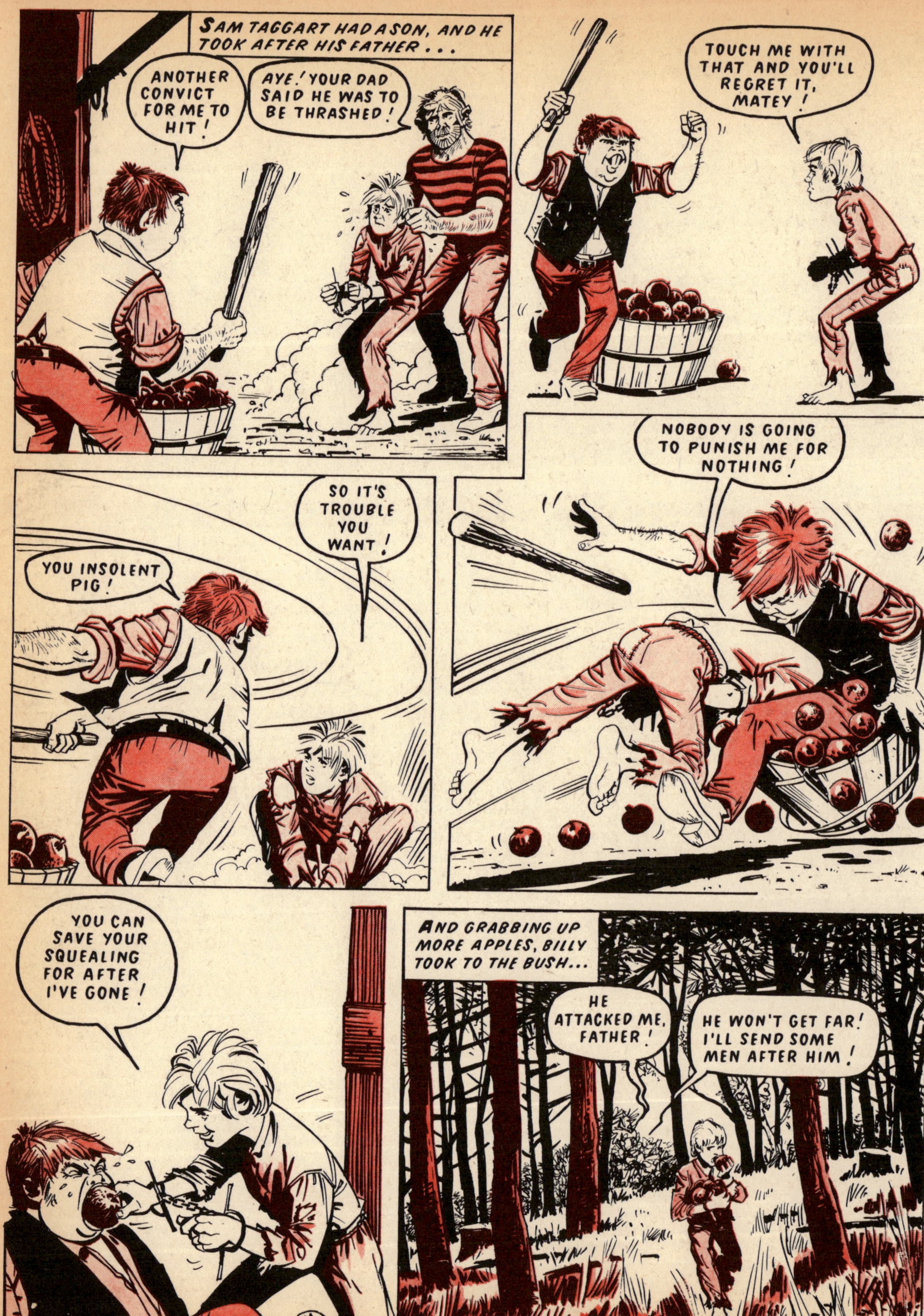
SAM TAGGART HAD A SON, AND HE TOOK AFTER HIS FATHER . . .
ANOTHER CONVICT FOR ME TO HIT!
AYE! YOUR DAD SAID HE WAS TO BE THRASHED!
TOUCH ME WITH THAT AND YOU'LL REGRET IT, MATEY!
YOU INSOLENT PIG!
SO IT'S TROUBLE YOU WANT!
NOBODY IS GOING TO PUNISH ME FOR NOTHING!
YOU CAN SAVE YOUR SQUEALING FOR AFTER I'VE GONE!
AND GRABBING UP MORE APPLES, BILLY TOOK TO THE BUSH...
HE ATTACKED ME, FATHER!
HE WON'T GET FAR! I'LL SEND SOME MEN AFTER HIM!

THE HUNT WENT ON FOR A NIGHT AND A DAY AND THEY MIGHT HAVE CAUGHT BILLY BUT FOR BOOMER THE BIG KANGAROO . . .
HEY! LOOK AT THE SIZE OF THAT KANGAROO!
LET'S GET AFTER IT! GOOD MEAT WILL GIVE US THE STRENGTH TO CHASE THAT BOY!

BILLY WAITED IN HIDING UNTIL THE MEN WERE GONE . . .
BUT FOR THAT KANGAROO THEY'D HAVE SURELY CAUGHT ME! I HOPE IT GETS AWAY!

LATER THAT EVENING . . .
IT'S THE SAME KANGAROO! IT DID MANAGE TO EVADE THEM, TOO!

BILLY SHOULD HAVE PUSHED ON, BUT HE STAYED WITH THE INJURED ANIMAL . . .
I'M SORRY, OLD MATE! BUT IT'S THE BEST I CAN DO! I HOPE YOU'RE MORE COMFORTABLE NOW!

BILLY'S STRANGE WAY WITH ANIMALS WORKED WITH THE KANGAROO, TOO, FOR WHEN BILLY SET OFF AT DAWN THE FOLLOWING MORNING . . .
CRUMBS! HE'S COMING WITH ME!

EVEN WHEN OTHER KANGAROOS APPEARED ON THE LANDSCAPE, THE BIG ANIMAL STAYED WITH BILLY . . .
I APPRECIATE THE COMPANY, BUT YOU MIGHT END UP IN TROUBLE IF YOU STAY WITH ME!

SOME WEEKS AFTER BILLY'S ESCAPE, A TRADER RETURNED FROM THE BUSH MUCH RICHER THAN HE WENT INTO IT. BESIDES THE NUGGET OF GOLD, HE HAD A STRANGE TALE TO TELL . . .
I GOT IT FROM A CONVICT KID IN PAYMENT FOR REMOVING HIS IRONS!
DID HE TELL YOU WHERE HE GOT IT FROM?
NEVER GOT THE CHANCE TO ASK! AS SOON AS THE IRONS WERE OFF SO WAS HE—ON THE BACK OF A BIG KANGAROO!
BILLY AND BOOMER LIVED ON IN THE BUSH AND TOGETHER THEY SURVIVED...
SWERVE TO THE RIGHT, BOOMER! THERE'S ANOTHER ONE COMING!
IT WASN'T LONG BEFORE BILLY COULD THROW A BOOMERANG, TOO . . .
HOW'S THAT, BOOMER?
AND SO THE FRIENDSHIP GREW . . .
IT WAS WORTH GETTING CONVICTED AND SHIPPED OUT HERE JUST TO MEET UP WITH YOU!

THEN ONE AFTERNOON WHILE WATCHING KOALA BEARS . . .
SNIFF
WHAT IS IT, BOOMER? SMELL SOMETHING NEAR? IF IT'S A DINGO I'LL SOON CLOBBER HIM WITH MY BOOMERANG!

THEN BILLY SAW THE MEN ON THE SKYLINE . . .
CRIPES! IT'S TAGGART! COME ON, BOOMER — LET'S GO!

THERE HE IS, DAD!
AFTER HIM, MEN! REMEMBER I WANT HIM ALIVE!

KEEP GOING, BOOMER! I KNOW HOW WE'LL LOSE 'EM!

NOT DOWN THERE, MASSA!
IGNORE HIM! GET AFTER THEM!

A MOMENT LATER, TAGGART WAS TO REGRET HIS DECISION . . .
THEIR HORSES AREN'T SO SURE-FOOTED AS YOU, BOOMER! WE'VE TRAPPED THEM IN THE SKREE!

TAGGART MEANT TO TAKE IT OUT ON SOMEONE FOR HIS OWN BLUNDER. HE CHOSE THE ABORIGINE TRACKER...
THANKS TO YOU WE'VE LOST OUR HORSES AND MOST OF OUR RATIONS! I'M GOING TO PUNISH YOU HARD FOR THAT!
LET ME THRASH HIM, DAD!

HARDLY HAD THE WRETCHED BOY SPOKEN, WHEN...
WHAT THE..?

LET HIM GO!
DO AS HE SAYS, DAD!

TAGGART DID AS BILLY ORDERED...
TAKE US TO WHERE YOU FOUND THE GOLD, AND I WILL SEE YOU GET YOUR FREEDOM!
I'VE GOT ALL THE FREEDOM I NEED! GO BACK WHERE YOU CAME FROM AND LEAVE ME BE!

THAT WAS THE LAST BILLY WAS TO SEE OF THE TYRANT TAGGART BUT IT WAS NOWHERE NEAR THE END OF THE INCIDENT...
LET'S TRACK DOWN ONE OF THEIR PACK ANIMALS. THERE SHOULD BE PLENTY OF FOOD FOR US TO EAT!

BUT OTHERS HAD GOT THERE FIRST...
THOSE ABORIGINES DON'T MISS A THING! LOOKS LIKE WE'LL BE LIVING OFF THE BUSH AGAIN!

BUT INSTEAD OF RUNNING, THE MEN STARTED CHEERING...

CRUMBS! THEY'RE NOT RUNNING! LOOKS LIKE I'VE GOT YOU IN TROUBLE THIS TIME, BOOMER!

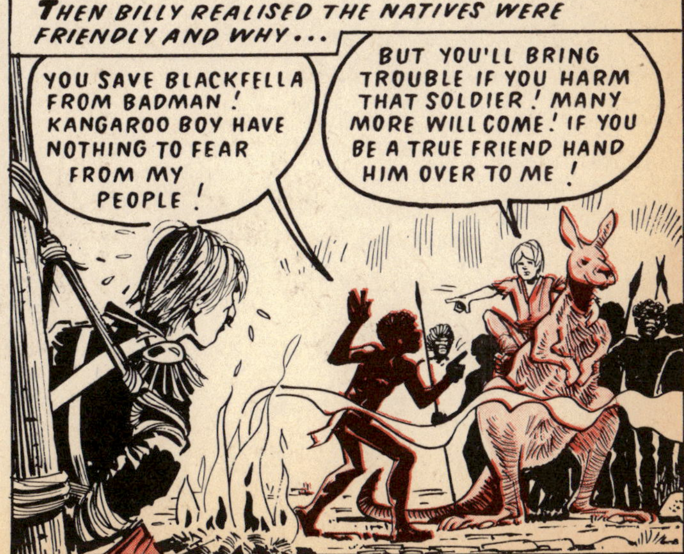

WE FOUND THIS IN THE CREEK ALONG WITH THE OTHER BIT! TAKE IT FOR A WEDDING PRESENT FROM BOOMER AND ME!

GOLD! THIS IS WORTH A FORTUNE!

THE SOLDIER WENT BACK TO THE SETTLEMENT, BUT LATER RETURNED TO FIND BILLY . . .

IT'S A PARDON FROM THE GOVERNOR, BOOMER! I'M FREE TO GO AS I PLEASE!

THAT'S RIGHT. HE HEARD HOW YOU SAVED MY LIFE! NOW YOU CAN COME BACK AND LIVE WITH US AND THERE'S PLENTY OF ROOM FOR BOOMER, TOO!

The Toffs and the Toughs
IT'S NICE TO HEAR CHRISTMAS CAROLS! PITY WE HAVEN'T GOT ANY CHRISTMAS FOOD TO GO WITH THEM! SIGH!
GOOD KING WENCESLAS LOOKED OUT

BOOM!
AS IT'S CHRISTMAS, WE'VE DECIDED TO GIVE YOU TOUGHS A PRESENT!
WOW! THANKS, TOFFS!

SORRY THEY'RE A BIT STALE! THEY WERE LEFT OVER FROM LAST YEAR! CHUCKLE!
OH, NO! THE TOFFS HAVE DONE IT AGAIN!
CRASH!
SMASH!
THUD!

GRR! WE'LL SCALE THE WALLS WITH OUR LADDERS! THEY HAVE FORGOTTEN THEIR MOAT'S FROZEN OVER!
HO, HO! NO WE HAVEN'T...!
BANG!
BANG!

ONE SUPER TOFF SNOWBALL COMING UP!
TEE, HEE! I CAN'T WAIT TO SEE THE LOOK ON THEIR FACES...!

HO, HO! YOU CAN'T EVEN SEE THEIR FACES! CHUCKLE!
ZOOM!
SPLAT!
SPLODGE!

HO, HO! THE TOUGHS AREN'T PLAYING... WE'LL PLAY SNOWMEN INSTEAD! CHUCKLE!
PLOP!
PLOP!
ZING!
ZING!
PLOP!
ZING!

GRR! WE'LL GET YOU FOR THAT, TOFFS..!
HO, HO! DO YOUR WORST, TOUGHS!

YAH! YOU MISSED US, TOUGHS!
TEE, HEE! WE'RE NOT AIMING FOR THE TOFFS THIS TIME...!
PLOP! PLOP!
ZOOM!

GRR! NOW WE'LL HAVE A GAME OF CANNONBALLS! TITTER!
CHUCKLE! WAIT FOR IT!

GASP! WHAT HAPPENED..?
TEE, HEE! OUR SNOWBALLS MELTED INSIDE THE TOFFS' CANNON JUST AS WE PLANNED!
SIZZLE!
PHUT!
CRUNCH!

HO, HO! THANKS FOR PROVIDING US WITH A NEW HOME, TOFFS!
BAH! WE'LL SEE ABOUT THAT!

AND SOON...
SIGH! THIS IGLOO MAKES A SMASHING WINTER HOME!
WAIT A MINUTE! THE ROOF'S LEAKING ALREADY!
DRIP!

FAN HEATER
FAN HEATER
BAH! IT WASN'T A LEAK! IT WAS THE TOFFS!
HO, HO! THERE'S MORE THAN ONE WAY TO TURN THE FIRE ON THE TOUGHS!

IT'S NO USE! THERE'S NOT ENOUGH LEFT TO BUILD A NEW HUT! WE'LL HAVE TO MOVE SOMEWHERE ELSE!
CHUCKLE! WE'LL GET READY TO FOLLOW THEM!

CHUCKLE! WE'LL GET OUR OWN BACK ON THOSE TOFFS WITH SOME CATAPULTS OF OUR OWN!

WHEEE!
POING!
ZOOM!

YIKES! THE TOUGHS HAVE GONE ALREADY!
NEVER MIND! THEY'VE LEFT THEIR TRACKS IN THE SNOW... WE'LL SOON CATCH THEM ON OUR SKIS!

BUT...
GASP! THEY'VE DISAPPEARED INTO THIN AIR! THE TRACKS HAVE STOPPED!

HO, HO! WE WALKED BACK ACROSS THE SNOW WITH OUR BOOTS ON BACK TO FRONT! CHUCKLE!
OH, NO! THEY WERE THERE ALL THE TIME!

HEAT!
WE'VE GOT ALL THE FOOD WE WANT, NOW! BUT WE CAN'T HAVE OUR CAROLS!
WAIT A MINUTE... PERHAPS I CAN PERSUADE THE TOFFS TO HELP OUT!
CHATTER!
SHIVER!

AND SOON...
AH... THAT MUST BE THEM, NOW..!
KNOCK! KNOCK!

HO, HO! KEEP SINGING FOR YOUR SUPPER, TOFFS! IT'S OUR TURN TO CALL THE TUNE, NOW! CHUCKLE!
BAH! GOOD KING WENCESLAS LOOKED OUT... GRR!
CAROLS
CAROLS

Joker's Jokes

Joker

YOU'D BETTER NOT HAVE ANY OF YOUR JOKES IN THAT SATCHEL, JOKER, OUR NEW TEACHER'S A REAL BULLY!
YEAH, HE EVEN GAVE ME A HUNDRED LINES FOR SNEEZING WHILE HE WAS TALKING!
SCHOOL

I'VE A COUPLE OF GAGS HERE THAT WILL SETTLE HIM!
A SQUIRT CAMERA AND A JACK-IN-THE-BOX! WOW! YOU'RE REALLY ASKING FOR IT!

HOW DARE YOU BRING YOUR SILLY PRACTICAL JOKES INTO MY CLASSROOM!

I'M GOING TO SEND FOR THE HEADMASTER AND GET YOU INTO REAL TROUBLE!
HO, HO! I THOUGHT HE'D DO THAT!

JOKER SQUIRTED ME WITH THAT CAMERA, THEN WHEN I LOOKED TO SEE IF HE HAD ANY MORE JOKES IN HIS DESK, THE JACK-IN-THE-BOX HIT ME IN THE EYE!
COO, THE FIBBER!

IT COULDN'T HAVE HAPPENED LIKE SIR SAYS — THEY'RE NOT WHAT HE THINKS!
NONSENSE — THIS IS A SQUIRT CAMERA IF EVER I SAW ONE!

GROUGH!
YES... BUT IT'S GOT A REVERSE FIRING ACTION, SIR!
GULP!
SQUIRT!

SO HE SQUIRTED YOU WITH THIS CAMERA, DID HE?
ER, I MUST HAVE MADE A MISTAKE! BUT HE HIT ME WITH THIS, HEADMASTER!

I'LL SHOW YOU!

ARRGH! I SUPPOSE YOU THINK THAT'S FUNNY!
OH, CRUMBS!
BOK!
CLICK!
POING!

YOU'RE FIRED! ONE JOKER IN THIS SCHOOL IS QUITE ENOUGH!
HO, HO! LOOKS LIKE THE ALTERATIONS I MADE TO THOSE OLD GAGS ARE GOING TO LEAD TO CHANGES IN THE TEACHING STAFF!

SON
OF
SIR

HURRY, LADS! IT'S NEARLY NINE O'CLOCK!
I HAVEN'T SEEN SON YET! I BET HE'S LATE, AS USUAL...!

WRONG, BOYS! I'M HERE! SNIGGER!
YEEARRGH!

GRR! WE'LL BASH SON FOR THAT!
TITTER! I DON'T THINK SO, BOYS!

MEET MY BODYGUARD! MY DAD'S GIVING HIM POCKET MONEY TO PROTECT ME AGAINST YOU LOT!
ERK! IT'S BASHER!

SEE 'EM OFF, BASHER!
SNARL! GNASH!
HELP! KEEP HIM OFF!

AND SO...
SNIGGER! YOU'RE LATE, BOYS! TAKE THAT!
OUCH! THIS IS ALL SON'S FAULT!

SOON...
WE'LL GET... EVEN ... WITH SON!
YIKES! THEY'RE GOING TO BASH ME DURING BREAK! I'D BETTER GET BASHER!

I CAN HEAR THE BOYS ROUND THE CORNER, BASHER!
HAW, HAW! THEY WON'T KNOW WHAT HIT 'EM..!

GNNG! WHAT HIT ME..?

HO, HO! WE SAID, "WE'LL GET AN EVEN BIGGER BOY TO DEAL WITH SON!"
GRR! THAT'S NOT WHAT SON TOLD ME..!
OOER...!

TAKE THAT!
OUCH! STOPPIT!
TEE, HEE! LOOKS LIKE SON'S HAVING A SLIGHT "MISUNDERSTANDING" WITH BASHER! CHUCKLE!

Sammy Shrink

CHATTER!
CHATTER!
COO! THEY LOOK COLD! I THINK I'LL BUILD THEM A BIRD HOUSE!

NOW, LET ME SEE... WHAT CAN I USE FOR A LITTLE HOUSE..?

TEN MINUTES LATER . . .
YOU'LL BE ALL RIGHT, MONTY — YOU'RE INDOORS!
MONTY'S HOUSE
BUMP!

COOEE, BIRDIES!

THERE YOU ARE, BIRDIES!... I'LL SOON HAVE YOU UP IN THAT TREE!

PHEW! NOW I CAN GO INDOORS TO BED!

EEK! A SQUATTER!
SNORE
CIGARS

GET OUT OF MY BED!
BUT Y-YOU PINCHED MINE!

GRRR! I'LL GET MY OWN BACK!

THANKS FOR YOUR HELP, BROTHERS!
SSHHH!— QUIETLY DOES IT!
CIGARS

YEAH! WE'LL GIVE THE LITTLE CHEAT A BIG SURPRISE!

QUICK! BACK IN AND SHUT THE DOOR!

S L A M
HELP! WH-WHAT'S H-HAPPENING?

I'M LOCKED OUT! AND I'LL NEVER WAKE MUM AND DAD AT THIS TIME OF NIGHT!

SHIVER! TREMBLE!

THERE IS ONLY ONE THING FOR IT . . .
GRRR! WAIT TILL I GET BACK INDOORS!
DON'T GRUMBLE, SAMMY! IT'S LOVELY AN' COSY IN HERE!

DEAD EYE
of the
SUPER SEVEN

HI, DEAD EYE! MEANIE MUGGINS WON'T LET US IN TO SING A CAROL!
CHUCKLE! THAT'S NO PROBLEM, KIDS..!
NO CAROL SINGERS

YOU CAN SING FROM HERE... I'LL JUST GET OLD MEANIE TO THE FRONT DOOR! CHUCKLE!
PRESS
ZING!
GOOD KING WENCESLAS...

...LOOKED OUT..!
ARE YOU GOING TO GIVE THEM SOMETHING?
GRR! YOU BET, I AM..!

TAKE THAT! NOW LEAVE ME IN PEACE TO WATCH MY TELLY!
GLUB! TAKE COVER, KIDS! HE'S NEARLY AS GOOD AS DEAD EYE!
SPLAT!
SPLOOSH!
NO CAROL SINGERS

BAH! IT'S NO USE! HE'LL NEVER LET YOU SING A CAROL WHILE HIS TELLY'S ON!
GASP! DEAD EYE'S GIVEN UP!

MOMENTS LATER...
OH, NO! MY TELLY'S GONE WRONG!
CRACKLE
BUZZ
??

HEY, MISTER! IF YOU GIVE THE KIDS SOMETHING FOR THEIR CAROL, I'LL FIX YOUR TELLY!
EH..? OKAY, KID!

GRR... HERE YOU ARE, KIDS! HEY, WHERE ARE YOU GOING..?
TEE, HEE! I'M GOING TO FIX YOUR TELLY AS I PROMISED...!

BULL'S EYE! CHUCKLE! IT'LL WORK OKAY NOW, MISTER!
BONK!
ZING!
TURN!

GASP! IT'S WORKING PERFECTLY! B-BUT HOW DID YOU KNOW YOUR PELLET WOULD DO THE TRICK..?
TEE, HEE! THAT'S EASY, MISTER...!

...THAT'S HOW I TURNED THE AERIAL ROUND IN THE FIRST PLACE!
OH, NO! I'VE BEEN HAD!

TUT, TUT! WHAT A TEMPER! I'D BETTER REMIND HIM IT'S THE SEASON OF GOODWILL! CHUCKLE!
PING!
TEE, HEE! I THINK HE GOT THE MESSAGE, DEAD EYE!
PLOP
PLOP

Cooky

LOOK AFTER YOUR COUSIN HORACE, COOKY, WHILE I GO SHOPPING!
PANTRY

I'LL MAKE HIM SOME BANGERS AND MASH!
INSTANT MASH

HEY! WHERE HAVE THE BANGERS GONE?

!
OH, NO!

THEY'RE RUINED... AND I NEEDED THEM FOR YOUR DINNER, TOO!

THAT'S THE IDEA, HORACE!

Beat your Neighbour

WE'VE BEEN WATCHING 'SKY BY STARLIGHT' WITH PATRICK MOON!

WE'RE DOING EVEN BETTER—WE'RE SEEING THE STARS FOR OURSELVES!

HA, HA! BET WE SEE MORE STARS WITH OUR ASTRONOMICAL TELESCOPE!

BUT THEN...
HAW, HAW! YOU'RE RIGHT—YOU ARE SEEING MORE STARS!
GNFF!

COO! LOOK, DAD... THEY'RE BUILDING A GIANT TELESCOPE OBSERVATORY!
TWO CAN PLAY THAT GAME, SON!

BET OURS IS READY FIRST!
YOU STARTED FIRST!

HERE IS A NEWS FLASH! TWO METEORS HAVE JUST BEEN SIGHTED OVER THE BRITISH ISLES!
COO! HEAR THAT?
BET WE SEE THEM BEFORE YOU!

WHAT THEY SAW...
QUICK, DAD!
HURRY UP!
WAHAY! THERE IT IS... GOING EAST TO WEST!
NO IT'S NOT— IT'S GOING WEST TO EAST!

YEOW!
OH, NO!
KRASH!
CRUMBLE!

WH-WHAT HAPPENED?
BOTH OUR TELESCOPES HAVE GONE WEST!

THE GROUP
BRAIN
LUVVY
FATSO
STUPID
SHORTY
RINGO

YAHOO! THERE'S A COWBOY FILM ON AT THE RITZ!
I WONDER IF THEY KEEP THE HORSES IN THE STALLS? HEH, HEH!

RITZ CINEMA
GUN
XAN
PAY DESK
HOLD IT!
SCREEECH!

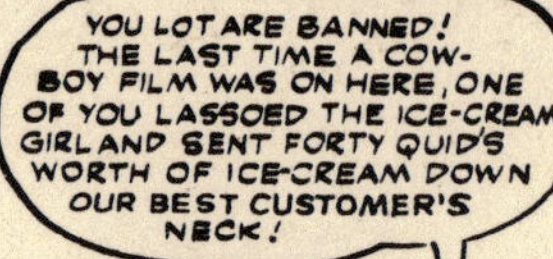
YOU LOT ARE BANNED! THE LAST TIME A COWBOY FILM WAS ON HERE, ONE OF YOU LASSOED THE ICE-CREAM GIRL AND SENT FORTY QUID'S WORTH OF ICE-CREAM DOWN OUR BEST CUSTOMER'S NECK!

GRR! WE AREN'T GOING TO MISS THE TWO-GUN TEXAN FOR ANYBODY!
IMAGINE HAVING A SHERIFF GUARDING THE PICTURES!

LEAVE HIM TO ME, LADS - I'LL GET HIM OUT OF THE WAY!

THAT LOT NEVER TAKE NO FOR AN ANSWER!

SNIP!
IT JUST SO HAPPENS I BORROWED THE CENSOR'S SCISSORS THIS MORNING!

AGGH! THE ROTTEN TWERP'S CUT MY LASSO! HE'S RUINED IT! WAA-AAH!
H'MM! MAYBE MY SHERIFF'S STAR WILL DO THE TRICK!
STOMP!

ONE SHERIFF'S STAR COMING UP! SNIGGER! SNIGGER!

AAAGH!
KTAK!

YAHOO! HE'S GONE! IN WE GO, LADS!
RITZ CINEMA
GUN
EXAN
PAY DESK
FOUR FOR THE STALLS, PLEASE! HEH, HEH!
ZOOM!

CINEMA
WHAT GOES UP-MUST COME DOWN!
GRR! IF HE HADN'T BEEN SO FAT HE WOULD HAVE TAKEN LONGER TO COME DOWN!
GRR! WE AIN'T FINISHED YET!

STOP THIEVES! THEY'VE NICKED MY HORSE!
I RECKON WE'D MAKE MIGHTY FINE RUSTLERS!
NOW LET'S RUSTLE UP SOME CINEMA TICKETS! HEH, HEH!

THUNDERING HOOVES
RIT
AGGH! THEY'RE BACK - THEY'RE GOING TO BURST THEIR WAY IN!

IT JUST SO HAPPENS I ALWAYS CARRY A CARROT AROUND WITH ME FOR SUCH AN EMERGENCY!

A CARROT FOR DOBBIN! SNIGGER!
TOSS!

YEOW! A LOVELY JUICY CARROT! THIS IS MY LUCKY DAY!
SCREECH!

WAA-AAH! THAT TWERP'S DONE IT AGAIN!
GREEDY OLD HOSS! ALWAYS THINKING OF ITS STOMACH!
WHEEEE!

IT TAKES MORE THAN A FEW BRAINLESS KIDS TO GET PAST ME!

THUMP!
COO! REVENGE! WELL-AIMED, HOSS!
RIGHT ON THE NUT!

RITZ CINEMA
O-GUN TEXAN.
PAY DESK
YAHOO! WE'RE IN-FOUR IN THE STALLS, PLEASE!
MIKE BROWN

COO! WHO INVITED HIM?
YIPPEE! THE TWO-GUN TEXAN'S GOT THE BADDIES!
EXIT
EXIT

MOOSE

OH, OH! FRENCHY LAFEET'S AFTER ME AGAIN!
STOP, MOOSE! ZERE IS NO ESCAPE!

HANDS ...ER... ANTLERS UP!

AND KEEP ZEM UP!

NOW, 'AVE YOU ZE LAST REQUEST, MOOSE?

"SNOW" THANK YOU... I'M OFF!
SPLAT!

SPIKE and TOOTS

SLOBBER!

CRUNCH!
CRUNCH!

YAP!
YAP!
YAP!

GROWL!
BARK!
SNARL!

CRUNCH!
MUNCH!

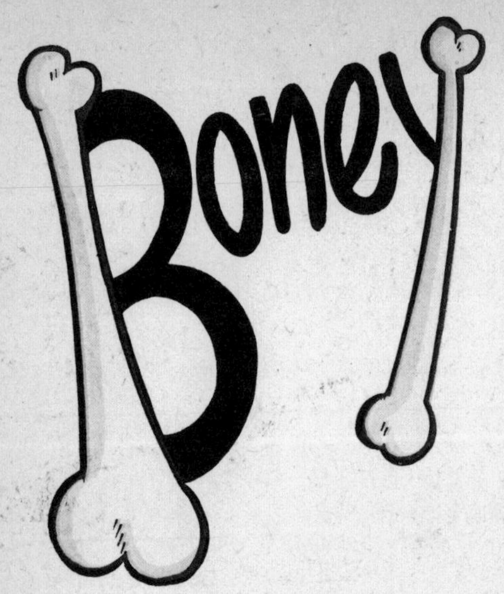
Boney

'GRAND FISHING CONTEST'
HOPE YOU DO WELL IN THE COMPETITION, BILLY!
YES—IT WOULD BE NICE TO WIN THE CUP!

HO, HO! YOU DON'T STAND A CHANCE, SON! WHY DON'T YOU SAVE YOURSELF THE EFFORT?
GRRR!
PAY NO ATTENTION, BILLY!

STAND BACK, BONEY—I'M GOING TO CAST!

WOW! STEADY, BILLY!
SWISH!
COIL!
ERK! SORRY, BONEY!
HEE, HEE! TOLD YOU!

TUG!
TOPPLE!
MAYBE I CAN PULL IT FREE..!
NO, BILLY... YAAGH!

OOER! POOR BONEY!
ZIZZZZZ!
HAW, HAW! THAT'LL BE ALL YOU'LL GET ON THE END OF YOUR LINE TODAY!
SPLOOOSH!

I'D BETTER PULL HIM IN FAST!
WHIRRR!

YANK!

PHEW! THANK GOODNESS YOU'RE SAFE, BONEY!
SPLUTTER! I'VE GOT SOMETHING FOR YOU, BILLY..!

HERE—IT GOT TRAPPED IN MY RIBS AS YOU PULLED ME IN!
COO! WHAT A WHOPPER!

SO...
THIS IS THE WINNER—CONGRATULATIONS, LAD!
BAH!
YIPPEE!
1ST
HEE, HEE! THAT'LL TEACH THEM TO RIB YOU, BILLY!

MY
BROVVER!

DOES LITTL'UN HAVE TO HELP ME CLEAR THE SNOW OFF THE PATH, MUM?
YES, HE DOES, LEN!

BAH! YOU'RE NO HELP, LITTL'UN! GO AND BUILD A SNOWMAN OR SOMETHING..!
TEE, HEE! OKAY, LEN..!

BUT...
WHAT THE..? YOU CAN'T MAKE A SNOWMAN WITH WATER, LITTL'UN!
TEE, HEE! YES I CAN!

GIVE ME THAT HOSE... YIKES! THE WATER'S FROZEN! ARRGH!

YEEOUCH!
CHUCKLE! WAIT FOR IT!

WHOOSH!
YIPPEE! ME MADE A SMASHING SNOWMAN AFTER ALL, LEN! TITTER!

GRR! I WON'T LET THINGS SLIDE AFTER THAT, LITTL'UN!
CHUCKLE! ME MAKE QUICK GETAWAY ON LEN'S SLEDGE..!

THAT DOES IT! YOU'VE BUSTED MY SLEDGE! SEETHE!
OOPS!

YOUR ESCAPE PLAN HAS "FALLEN THROUGH", LITTL'UN! PREPARE FOR A WHACKING..!
OOER..!

YELP! STOPPIT!
NOT YET, LITTL'UN! I'M ONLY JUST WARMING UP!

AND...
HO, HO! WE'LL SOON HAVE THE SNOW MELTED NOW LITTL'UN'S IN THE "HOT SEAT"! THAT'LL TEACH HIM TO "CLEAR OFF"! CHUCKLE!
BAH! OUCH!

Pete's Pockets

WAAA-AAH!
OH, NO! I'LL BE IN MORE TROUBLE NOW!

PHEW! WELL DONE, POCKETS! THEY'RE GOING TO CUSHION CRUMP'S FALL!

PHEW! THAT SHOULD PLEASE CONSTABLE CRUMP, ANYWAY!
SPLUMP!

NEEYAAGH!
SKREEEEEEEK!
OH, NO! THEY WERE SQUEAKY CUSHIONS!

SUFFERING SERGEANTS! THERE'S PUFFER PERKINS BLOWING A SAFE IN THERE!

WELL DONE, PETE! CATCHING CROOKS IS WHAT MAKES OUR JOB ALL WORTH WHILE!
BAH!
I MIGHT HAVE A... ER ... STAB AT IT MYSELF WHEN I GROW UP, CONSTABLE! HO, HO!
THROB! THROB!

SON of SIR

PLAYTIME ...
YIPPEE! THIS IS GREAT FUN!
MY TURN NEXT!
HEY! YOU BOYS..!

YOU'RE NOT ALLOWED TO SLEDGE IN THE SCHOOL GROUNDS! I'LL HAVE THAT SLEDGE!
BAH! YES, SIR!

HEE, HEE! NOW YOU CAN HAVE A GO, SON!
THANKS, DAD!
GRR! THAT'S NOT FAIR!

WOW!
OOH! CAREFUL, SON— DON'T WANT YOU GETTING HURT!
KRUNK!
YERK! NEVER MIND THAT—WHAT ABOUT OUR SLEDGE?

BAH! IT WON'T RUN STRAIGHT NOW!
I THINK THE BOYS ARE ANNOYED, SON —YOU'D BETTER SEE IF THEY'RE PLOTTING ANYTHING!
OKAY, DAD!

...HEAD...RUN...
SLEDGE...DAMAGE
SON AND SIR...
WOW! I'D BETTER WARN DAD!

DAD! THEY'RE GOING TO FIND THE HEAD AND RUN HIM DOWN WITH THEIR SLEDGE, THEN BLAME IT ON THE DAMAGE WE DID TO IT!
GASSP! WE MUST STOP THEM, SON!

HERE THEY COME, SON! WE'LL STOP THEM BEFORE THEY FIND THE HEAD... PULL!
RUMBLE!

GULP! IT IS THE HEAD!
GOT YOU... WOW!
YAAAGH!

GRRR! SNARL!
ERK! WE THOUGHT THE BOYS WERE GOING TO RUN YOU DOWN WITH THEIR SLEDGE, HEADMASTER, SIR!
HEE, HEE! SILLY SON AND SIR...

WAAAGH!
HEEELP!
ROARR! WAIT TILL I CATCH YOU!
...WE SAID, "WE'LL OFFER THE HEAD A RUN ON OUR SLEDGE AFTER WE'VE FIXED THE DAMAGE SON AND SIR CAUSED"!

BEAT YOUR NEIGHBOUR

HAVE YOU GOT THE BAKER'S WIFE?
HEE, HEE! MY DAD'S GREAT AT HAPPY FAMILIES!
HUH! THAT'S A KID'S GAME!

WE'RE GOING TO PLAY SNAP! IT'S A MUCH BETTER GAME!
YAH! THAT'S EASY!

SO... SNAP!
ERK! I CAN'T CONCENTRATE FOR ALL THAT NOISE!
NEVER MIND — I'VE GOT A BETTER IDEA..!

FETCH MORE PACKS OF CARDS AND I'LL BUILD A CARD SKYSCRAPER!
HEE, HEE! BET YOUR DAD CAN'T DO THAT!

HURRY, DAD — I'VE BROUGHT YOU MORE CARDS!
FETCH THE STEPLADDER, SON — IT'S SO TALL, I CAN HARDLY REACH THE TOP!

I'LL NEED STEPS, TOO, SON !
COME ON, DAD— THEY'RE CATCHING UP !

I'LL SOON HAVE OURS AS TALL AS THEIRS !
THAT'S AS HIGH AS I CAN GET IT—YOU WON'T MANAGE THAT !
GRR! HERE'S SOMETHING YOU CAN'T DO..!

HUH! YOU'RE CHEATING! BET THOSE CARDS ARE ON A STRING!
GRR! NO THEY'RE NOT! YOU'LL BE SORRY FOR THAT..!
SHUFFLE!

OH, YEAH... OOOGH!
TAKE THAT... GNNN!
THUMP
THUMP!
STOP! LOOK OUT!

GAAH!
ERK!
THUD!
KRUMP!
OOPS!
YAARGH!

LATER...
I BROUGHT YOU A GET WELL CARD, DAD!
GROAN!
MOAN!
SNAP! I BROUGHT YOU A GET WELL CARD, TOO, DAD - BUT MINE IS BETTER!

Little Devil

GRR! COME HERE WHOEVER DID THIS, OR I'LL WHACK THE LOT OF YOU!
CHUCKLE! DON'T OWN UP!

RIGHT! YOU LOT ARE FOR IT!
YIPPEE! THERE'S NOTHING LIKE A MASS WHACKING!

YEEARRGH! THE POP'S FROZEN!
SLIP!
ZIP!

AHA! YOU'VE DECIDED TO OWN UP, HAVE YOU?
YEEOUCH! B-BUT...!
KER-ZONK!

HO, HO! LITTLE DEVIL THOUGHT HE HAD ME OVER A BARREL, BUT HE SLIPPED UP! CHUCKLE!
POP
WHACK! WHACK!
YEEOUCH! STOPPIT!

FUSS POT

BAH! I'M FUSSY ABOUT THE WEATHER WE HAVE FOR MY CHRISTMAS HOLIDAYS!
HO, HO! EVEN YOUR FUSSING CAN'T DO ANYTHING ABOUT THE WEATHER, FUSS POT!

BUT...
YES IT CAN! WE'RE GOING TO SUNNY AUSTRALIA FOR THE HOLIDAY! HURRY UP AND PACK!
GASP! WHY DIDN'T I KEEP QUIET?
SUNNY AUSTRALIA

AND SOON...
BAH! THOSE TICKETS COST ME A FORTUNE, FUSS POT!
CUSTOMS
TICKET OFFICE
STOP, FUSSING! WE'LL MISS OUR PLANE...!

THERE WE ARE, MISS! YOU'RE THROUGH!
SHRIEK! HOW DARE YOU DRAW ALL OVER MY BEST CASE!

GET IT OFF AT ONCE! FUSS, FUSS!
Y-YES, MISS!
OH, DEAR! WHAT'S SHE GOING TO BE LIKE ON THE PLANE...?

HO, HO! YOU'LL HAVE TO WAIT FOR YOUR SUNSHINE, FUSS POT! WE'D BETTER GO BACK HOME!
BAH! I'M NOT GOING ANYWHERE IN THIS WEATHER! FUSS!
ALL FLIGHTS CANCELLED DUE TO SNOW

WE'LL JUST HAVE TO STAY HERE FOR THE NIGHT!
OH, NO! FUSS POT'S BACK!

SO...
HURRY UP! I'M FUSSY ABOUT SPENDING THE NIGHT IN COMFORT!
SIGH! COMING, FUSS POT...

AFTER A NIGHT OF FUSSING...!
THEY'VE CLEARED THE RUNWAY, FUSS POT! YOU CAN TAKE OFF NOW!
GASP! I LEFT MY CASE OUTSIDE ALL NIGHT WITH THE TICKETS IN IT!

HO, HO! YOU'LL NEVER FIND IT UNDER ALL THAT SNOW, FUSS POT!
OH, NO!

WE MIGHT AS WELL GO HOME, MUM! I THINK FUSS POT'S TRYING TO GET TO AUSTRALIA ON HER OWN! CHUCKLE!
BAH! VERY FUNNY! FUSS, FUSS!

Joker's Jokes

The Toffs and the Toughs

Frame-up

At first glance the two pictures below appear to be identical—but look closer and you'll see that the bottom one has been "got at". The artist has made 10 crafty alterations from the top illustration . . . see if you can spot them. (Answers below)

Montmorency's tuft of hair, Lancelot's bow tie, TRUNDLE! bigger, black band on skittle, extra action effect line, more hair on bowler, no smile on Ruff, different shoes on Scruff, more shadow on hut, coloured door on hut.

BOOTER
of the
SUPER
SEVEN

COME ON, BOOTER! WE NEED AN EXPERT LIKE YOU!
CHUCKLE! OKAY, KIDS! EVEN A MEMBER OF THE SUPER SEVEN CAN RELAX SOMETIMES!

GOOD OLD BOOTER... I'LL GET THE BALL..!

BUT...
HAW, HAW! SORRY, KID! WE NEED A BALL!
GLOOP!
SQUIRT!
SPLOOSH!

BAH! DON'T WORRY, LADS! I'LL SOON GET IT BACK!
EH..?

WOW! WHAT A SWERVE SHOT!
SWERVE
BOOT!

GASP! EVEN THUNDERBALL WOULD BE PROUD OF THAT MARBLE-TYPE TRICK!
THERE WE ARE, LADS!
BOUNCE!
BONK!

HO, HO! WE CAN PLAY NOW, LADS! THOSE BULLIES HAVE GIVEN UP!

BUT...
HAW, HAW! NO WE HAVEN'T!
SIGH! I'D BETTER GET RID OF THEM FOR GOOD..!
SLURP!
SLURP!
SLURP!

SNIGGER! WHAT A WEAK SHOT! THAT WON'T DO US ANY HARM!
TEE, HEE! OH, NO..?
FLIP!

BANG ON TARGET! CHUCKLE!
ARRGH!
GLUB!
SPLOOSH!
PLOP!
WHOOSH!

HO, HO! BOOTER REALLY PUT THE DAMPER ON THEIR PLANS! CHUCKLE!
GLUB!
SPLOSH!
SQUELCH!
PLAY ON, LADS! CHUCKLE!
BIFF

SON OF SIR

BAH! I CAN'T SLEEP WHILE THE BOYS SCRATCH AROUND WITH THEIR PENS, DAD!
SCRAPE!
SCRATCH!
YIPPEE! THAT MEANS WE CAN'T DO THIS TEST!

BUT...
DON'T WORRY, SON! THE BOYS CAN WORK OUTSIDE IN THE PLAYGROUND!
OH, NO! IT'S FREEZING OUT THERE!

YOU CAN'T HEAR THE PENS SCRATCHING NOW, SON! SNIGGER!
NO, DAD — BUT IT'S TOO LIGHT IN THE CLASSROOM FOR ME TO GET TO SLEEP!

I'VE GOT AN IDEA — TAKE THAT, YOU LOT!
AARGH!

GRR! EVEN SIR'S NOT GOING TO STOP US GETTING OUR OWN BACK FOR THAT..!

TEE, HEE! THANKS, BOYS! THE ROOM'S NICE AND DARK NOW!
CHUCKLE! CARRY ON WORKING, BOYS! I WON'T TELL THE HEAD WHAT YOU'VE DONE UNTIL MY SON'S HAD A SLEEP!

BUT...
WE'LL GET... CLEAN... AWAY!
GASP! THEY'RE GOING TO ESCAPE! I'D BETTER GET DAD!

QUICK, DAD! THE BOYS ARE RUNNING AWAY!
GRR! I'D BETTER TELL THE HEAD ABOUT THEM NOW— HE'LL SOON STOP THEM..!

THE BOYS WERE JUST ROUND THIS CORNER, HEADMASTER! WE'LL SOON PICK UP THEIR TRAIL!

GASP! WHAT THE..?
ARRGH! GLUB!
HO, HO! I SAID, "WE'LL GET THE WINDOW CLEAN WHILE SIR'S AWAY"!

GRR! WHY DON'T YOU DO SOMETHING USEFUL LIKE THE BOYS!
HELP!
HO, HO! SON WON'T GET MUCH SLEEP NOW— SIR'S REALLY PUT HIS FOOT IN IT! CHUCKLE!

FUSS POT

EEEK! WHAT A NOISE! I'M FUSSY ABOUT SO MUCH DISTURBANCE OUTSIDE MY HOUSE!
SLAM!
THE MOTORISTS HAVE TO PARK SOMEWHERE, FUSS POT... AND THERE ARE DOUBLE YELLOW LINES ON THE OTHER SIDE OF THE STREET!

SIGH! NOW WHAT'S SHE UP TO?
FUSS, FUSS! SOMEBODY WILL PAY FOR THIS... HEY! THAT'S AN IDEA...!
VROOOM!

HELLO...IS THAT THE TOWN ROADS DEPARTMENT..? FUSS, FUSS!
OOER!

SOON...
THERE! I GOT THEM TO PUT UP A PARKING METER! AT £5 A TIME, NOBODY WILL BE ABLE TO AFFORD TO PARK OUTSIDE!
GASSP! B-BUT..!
£5 FOR 30 MINUTES

...YOU MIGHT HAVE WARNED DAD FIRST... HE DIDN'T KNOW IT WAS THERE!
KERRASH!
EEEK! I'M FUSSY ABOUT PEOPLE DAMAGING MY PROPERTY!
SWERVE!

FUSS, FUSS! TO MAKE UP FOR IT, YOU CAN PAINT DOUBLE YELLOW LINES ON THIS SIDE OF THE STREET! THAT'LL STOP ALL PARKING AND THE NOISE!
YOU'LL NEVER GET AWAY WITH THIS, FUSS POT!
YELLOW

GRR! NOW WHERE ARE THE MOTORISTS GOING TO PARK?
BLACK
YELLO

THEY CAN PARK ON THIS SIDE OF THE STREET... AFTER YOU'VE PAINTED OUT THE YELLOW LINES! FUSS, FUSS!
BUT... AW, WHAT'S THE USE?
BLACK

LOOK! IT'S WORKING!
H'MM! THEY'VE CHANGED THE SIDE WE'RE ALLOWED TO PARK ON!

BUT, LATER...
BRRRRM!
VRRROOOM!
YEEEEK! WHASSAT?
HEH, HEH! IT'S THE CARS YOU MADE PARK ON THE OTHER SIDE OF THE STREET..!

THEIR TYRES HAVE GOT STUCK ON THE WET PAINT...AND YOU'RE GOING TO HAVE TO GO AND HELP FREE THEM!
GAAAAH! THE NOISE IS WORSE THAN EVER!

The TOFFS...

BRR! CHRISTMAS EVE, AND WE HAVEN'T EVEN GOT ENOUGH WOOD FOR A FIRE!
TEE, HEE! WE'LL SOON FIX THAT, TOUGHS...!

FIRE!
BOOM!
BOOM!
OH, NO!

HO, HO! YOU'VE GOT PLENTY OF FIREWOOD NOW, TOUGHS!
SPLINTER!
CRUNCH!
CRASH!
GASP! OUR ROOF!

BAH! WE'LL HAVE TO FIND SOME WOOD FOR A NEW ROOF INSTEAD, NOW!
TEE, HEE! THEIR HUT IS JUST THE WAY WE WANT IT!

TEE, HEE! NOW WE CAN ORDER SOME MORE COAL!
IT MAKES A SUPER COAL-BUNKER! TITTER!
DELIVERIES FOR THE TOFFS HERE

AND...
HEY! YOU CAN'T DO THAT!
DELIVERIES FOR THE TOFFS HERE
WHOOSH!
TIP!
C. BLACK, COAL MERCHANT
TITTER! TOO LATE, TOUGHS! HE HAS!

and the TOUGHS

Sammy Shrink

DAD'S BOUGHT A PORTABLE TELLY, SO NOW I CAN LAY IN BED AND WATCH MY FAVOURITE PROGRAMME!

ERK! LOOK AT THAT!

THESE MICE ACT AS THOUGH THEY OWN THE PLACE!

GERROFF! YOU LITTLE PESTS!
EEK!

HEY WAIT A MINUTE! THEY'VE GIVEN ME AN IDEA!

HEY, MICE! YOU CAN WATCH MY TELLY!

GOTCHA!
HELP! IT'S A TRAP!

THE MOONSHINE BREAKFAST
O K! CHANGE THE CHANNEL! HEE, HEE! THIS SAVES ME GETTING OUT OF BED TO DO IT!

BUT—ENTER ONE TATTY OLD TOM...
COO! AN UNCHEWED GOB-STOPPER, YUM, YUM!

I'M FREE! SAVED BY A MOGGY! I DON'T BELIEVE IT!

LOOK OUT, LADS! I'M COMING THROUGH!
COME HERE! THINK YOU CAN GO ON STRIKE, DO YOU?

AAGH!

YOU CAN'T DO THIS TO ME! LET ME OUT!

BAH! ROTTEN LITTLE TWERPS! WAIT TILL I GET OUT OF HERE!
HOW'S THAT, THEN? WE'VE GOT COLOUR T V!

The
FULL HOUSE

MUM'S PLEASED TODAY BECAUSE DAD'S BOUGHT A NEW BEDROOM CARPET!

AND...
HO, HO! THERE'S NOTHING TO LAYING A CARPET WHEN YOU KNOW WHAT YOU'RE DOING!

WHAT THE..? ARRGH! THE TACKS HAVE COME OUT!
BONK!
ROLL!
TEE, HEE! GOOD OLD DAD! HE'S ENOUGH TO MAKE YOU ROLL UP!

GRR! YOU LOT CAN STAND ON THE CARPET THIS TIME, JUST TO MAKE SURE!
CHUCKLE! OKAY, DAD!

TOPPLE!
HELP!
SPRING!
ARRGH!

HO, HO! THAT'LL TEACH YOU LOT TO WRAP UP!
ROLL!
ERK!

LET'S TACKLE THIS JOB SENSIBLY — WE'LL PILE ALL THE HEAVY FURNITURE ON THE EDGE OF THE CARPET TO HOLD IT DOWN...!

BAH! I HOPE YOU LOT WILL HELP ME GET THE HOUSE STRAIGHT AFTER ALL THIS!
YOU BET, MUM! WE'VE GOT SOME FURNITURE FROM OUR ROOMS JUST TO MAKE SURE...!

RIGHT! THAT LOT SHOULD HOLD THE CARPET DOWN — WE'LL START UNROLLING IT NOW!
WAIT A MINUTE — I'VE BEEN MEANING TO STRAIGHTEN THAT PICTURE UP FOR AGES, AND NOW I CAN REACH...!

THAT'S ODD! THE PICTURE'S STRAIGHT NOW, BUT THE WINDOW'S CROOKED!
WHAT THE..?

OH, NO! WE MOVED TOO MUCH FURNITURE TO ONE SIDE!

Pete's Pockets

YAAGHH! WHAT'S HAPPENING DOWN THERE?
C-CRUMBS! MY DAFT POCKETS ARE TRYING THE SAME GAG AGAIN!
BOB'S CIRCUS

GERROUTOFFIT! SNIGGER!
HOWL! HOWL!
HEY! THAT WAS CRUEL, MISTER!
BOB'S CIRCUS
STAMP!
STAMP!

THERE! THAT SHOULD SOOTHE YOUR SORE FINGERS!
WAAAH! MY EYES MUST BE PLAYING TRICKS!
SOOTHING CREAM
SPLOB!
THROB!
THROB!

I'M GOING TO GET SOME HELP! GULP!

STONE THE CROWS! HE'S SLIPPED ON THE SOOTHING CREAM!
SLITHER!
CRACK!

THROB!
THROB!
SOOTHE!
SOOTHING CREAM
I SHOULDN'T REALLY SNEAK IN FOR NOTHING BUT HE WAS RATHER NASTY... WASN'T HE? HO, HO!
BOB'S CIRCUS
VERY NASTY, PETE! HEE, HEE!

SPIKE and TOOTS

MINE... ALL MINE!

?

?

Joker's Jokes

WINDY
of the
SUPER SEVEN

NO CALLS FOR HELP TODAY, SO I'LL TAKE A QUIET STROLL BY THE LAKE..!
BOATS FOR HIRE
3

BUT...
HELP, WINDY! OUR BUNG'S SHOT OUT!
WHOOOSH!
YIKES! I SPOKE TOO SOON! HANG ON, LADS..!
5

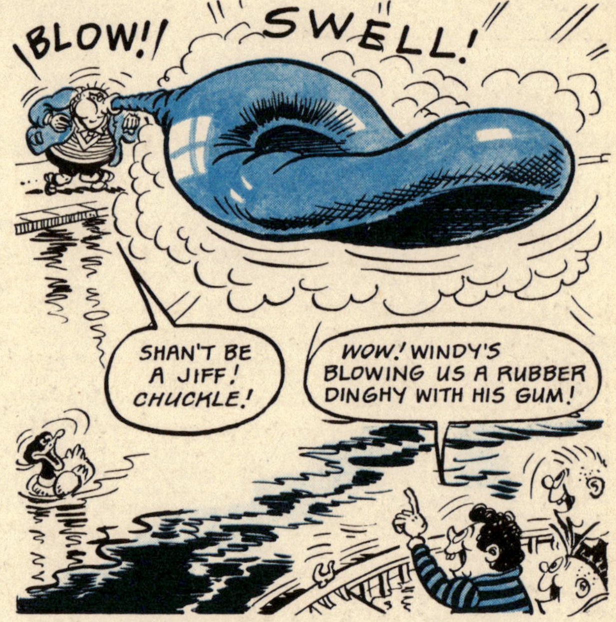
BLOW!
SWELL!
SHAN'T BE A JIFF! CHUCKLE!
WOW! WINDY'S BLOWING US A RUBBER DINGHY WITH HIS GUM!

PHEW! THANKS, WINDY!
SPLOSH!
HEAVE!
DON'T FORGET THE OARS, LADS!

I'LL KEEP HOLD OF THE ROPE SO WE CAN PULL THE BOAT ASHORE!

GIVE ME A HAND, LADS! WE'LL SOON HAVE YOUR BOAT ASHORE!
OKAY, WINDY! THERE'S ONLY ONE TROUBLE..!

...IT'S NOT OURS! IT BELONGS TO THE MAN ON THE OTHER SIDE OF THE LAKE, AND WE CAN'T GET IT BACK!
HO, HO! THAT'S NO TROUBLE AT ALL! STAND BACK..!

FIRST I'LL GET THE WATER OUT FAST!
WOW! BUT WE STILL HAVEN'T GOT A BUNG!
WHOOSH!
BLAST

LET ME WORRY ABOUT THAT! HELP ME TURN THE BOAT OVER, KIDS!
EH..? OKAY, WINDY!
HEAVE!

RIGHT! CLIMB ABOARD, LADS! AND HOLD TIGHT!
GASP! WHAT'S WINDY UP TO..?

YIPPEE! WINDY'S TURNED OUR BOAT INTO A HOVERCRAFT!
BLOW
HO, HO! TRUST WINDY TO "TURN UP" WITH SOMETHING!

THE GROUP
BRAIN
LUVVY
FATSO
STUPID
SHORTY
RINGO

HELLO, WHAT'S THIS SAY? "A PRESENT FOR P.C. FLATT'S LEFT FOOT — THE BIGGEST FOOT IN TOWN!"
A PRESENT FOR P.C. FLATT'S LEFT FOOT- THE BIGGEST FOOT IN TOWN

SOME PEOPLE THINK THEY'RE VERY FUNNY — MY FEET AREN'T **THAT** BIG!

AAGH! THAT BOOT LEAKS!

HEH, HEH! THAT'LL TEACH HIM NOT TO PINCH OUR CATAPULTS!
ZOOM!
GRR! I MIGHT HAVE KNOWN — IT'S THE GROUP!

GLAD I KNEW ABOUT THAT SHORTCUT! I'LL GET THEM NOW — THEY HAVEN'T HAD TIME TO FILL UP WITH WATER AGAIN!
ZIP!
ZIP!

ENEMY ATTACKING — PREPARE TO FIRE!

SPLUDGE!
FIRE! HEH! HEH! HOW'S THAT FOR A GUN?
A CAP GUN — A TOE CAP GUN!
BOOM!
SEMOLINA

GRR! THEY CAN'T HAVE ANY MORE SEMOLINA AND THAT'S FOR SURE — THAT THING MUST'VE BEEN OVERLOADED AS IT WAS!
RUMBLE RUMBLE!

WHO NEEDS SEMOLINA? HEH, HEH!
WINK!

ER-EK! WHAT'S HAPPENING?

BLAT!
HEH, HEH! THAT'S THE-ER-SOLE OF THE BOOT!
SORRY WE CAN'T PROVIDE CHIPS, TOO!

THEY WON'T INTIMIDATE ME — THEY AIN'T GETTING THEIR CATAPULTS BACK — EVER!

HEH, HEH! JUST IN CASE I'M TEMPTED, I'LL BURN THE LOT — THEN I CAN'T GIVE THEM BACK! CHUCKLE! CHUCKLE!
CONFISCATED CATAPULTS

WELL! HERE WE GO—!

AAGH! THEY'VE FILLED IT UP AGAIN!
WHOOSH!
WELL! THAT'S THE MATCH OUT — OUR CATAPULTS ARE SAFE NOW!

YAHOO! WE'VE GOT THEM BACK!
WE'RE ARMED AGAIN!
SNATCH!
ZOOM!
SCREECH!

GRR! I AIN'T BEATEN YET!
ZOOM

RUMBLE
GLUG! GLUG!
TWO CAN PLAY AT THEIR GAME — I'LL GIVE THEM SOME POLISH FOR THEIR BOOT! SNIGGER!

WAA-AAH! ABANDON BOOT!
SOS! MAYDAY!
SKID!
SKID!
SKID!
AAGH! SOMEONE'S BEEN POLISHING THE PAVEMENT!

OH, NO! IT'S HEADING FOR THAT FIRE!
DEMOLITION
A. RHODES
AND OUR CATAPULTS ARE WITH IT — STOP IT! STOP IT!
BUMP!
CRUNCH

BOO-HOO! NO CATAPULTS — AND NO BOOT NOW AS WELL! ROTTEN OLD P.C. FLATT! SOB! SOB!
P.C. FLATT DOES IT AGAIN!
CRACKLE!
CRACKLE!
CRACKLE

Beat your Neighbour

I'M GOING TO HAVE MY CAR CHROMIUM PLATED ALL OVER!

I EVEN HAD OUR ENGINE SILVER PLATED! YOU CAN'T BEAT THAT!

LOOK AT THE LOVELY PINK SMOKE FROM OUR NEW EXHAUST PIPES!
SPLUTTER!
CHOKE!

GANGWAY FOR OUR NEW WHEELS!
OW!
OOCH!

LET'S SHOW OFF OUR NEW-LOOK CAR!
WE'LL SHOW OFF MORE THAN YOU!
CREAK!
GROAN!

THEY'VE BEAT THEMSELVES TODAY-THE CARS HAVE COLLAPSED UNDER THE WEIGHT! HA, HA!
CRASH!
SHATTER!

JOKER

YERK! HERE COMES THAT AWFUL JOKER! HE'S BOUND TO CAUSE TROUBLE... UNLESS...!
PARK KEEPER

HEH, HEH! SORRY, LADS... YOU CAN'T PLAY HERE! THE POND NEEDS DRAINING!
BAH! IT'S NOT FAIR! THE POND'S OKAY — HE JUST WANTS TO GET RID OF ME BECAUSE HE THINKS I'LL PLAY SOME TRICKS ON HIM!
GURGLE!

DON'T WORRY, TOMMY... WE'RE NOT BEATEN YET, BUT I'LL HAVE TO NIP HOME FIRST!
?

LATER....
SWIMMING BATHS
JOKES AND TRICKS
OOER! JOKER'S COMING TO THE BATHS... AND HE'S BROUGHT A BIG BOX OF TRICKS TO PLAY ON US!

MAYBE HE'LL PUT DYE IN THE WATER!

BET HE TRIES TO SCARE US WITH A SCAREY MASK!

CHANGING CUBICLES
GASP! HE'LL SCATTER ITCHING POWDER ALL OVER THE CHANGING ROOMS!

SWIMMING BATHS
COME ON! LET'S BEAT IT BEFORE HE PLAYS SOME OF HIS PRANKS ON US!
JOKES AND TRICKS
HEE, HEE! WE'RE GOING TO HAVE THE PLACE TO OURSELVES! COME ON, TOMMY!

SOON....
I SAY...IT'S VERY QUIET THIS AFTERNOON! I'LL GO AND SEE IF THERE'S ANYONE IN AT ALL!
BATHS MANAGER

GASP!
HEE, HEE! THEY THOUGHT THAT BOX WAS FULL OF TRICKS...BUT IT WAS FULL OF ALL OUR TOY BOATS!
HEE, HEE! THE THOUGHT OF JOKER AND HIS JOKES SCARED THEM ALL AWAY! NOW WE'VE GOT ENOUGH ROOM FOR A WHOLE FLEET!
SHOWERS

SON of SIR

AS IT'S THE LAST DAY OF TERM, MY DAD'S ARRANGED FOR FATHER CHRISTMAS TO CALL, BOYS!
WOW! SIR CAN'T BE SO BAD, AFTER ALL!

THANK YOU, FATHER CHRISTMAS! TITTER!
COO! WE'RE GOING TO GET LOADS OF PRESENTS! LOOK WHAT HE'S GIVEN SON!

BUT...
AND HERE'S ONE FOR THE OTHER BOYS! SNIGGER!
GRR! WAIT A MINUTE! I RECOGNISE THAT VOICE!

BAH! IT'S SIR IN DISGUISE!
ERK! HOW DARE YOU PULL MY BEARD..!
TUG!

HELP! WHERE HAVE THEY GONE?
TWANG!
DON'T WORRY, DAD! I'LL CHASE THEM OFF..!

I'LL GO AND MAKE SURE THE BOYS DON'T GIVE MY SON ANY TROUBLE..!

SON'S GOING TO... CATCH... IT!
I MUST PROTECT MY DEAR SON..!

WAIT, DAD! I'M HERE!
HUH..?

YIKES! THE DOOR'S SLAMMED! I'VE LOCKED US OUT!
HUH..?
SLAM!
HO, HO! WE SAID, "SON'S GOING TO DROP THE CATCH ON THE DOOR SO WE CAN'T OPEN IT".

WHAT'S GOING ON? WHY HAVEN'T THE BOYS GOT THEIR PRESENTS?
OOER... THEY'RE LOCKED INSIDE THE SCHOOL, HEADMASTER! AND ALL THE WINDOWS ARE SHUT FOR THE HOLIDAYS!

GRR! IN THAT CASE, THERE'S ONLY ONE WAY IN! GRAB THAT LADDER!
OH, NO..!

BAH!
HURRY UP, SIR!
HO, HO! SIR'S REALLY ACTING LIKE FATHER CHRISTMAS, AFTER ALL!

FUSS POT

I'VE BROUGHT HOME A PICTURE! I'M FUSSY ABOUT HAVING A BIT OF CULTURE IN THE HOUSE!
ER... LET'S HAVE A LOOK AT IT, FUSS POT..!

GASP! WHAT IS IT?
TUT, TUT! FANCY NOT BEING ABLE TO SPOT A MASTERPIECE WHEN YOU SEE ONE!

I'LL... ER... HANG IT IN THE SPARE ROOM, FUSS POT..!
YOU'LL DO NO SUCH THING! FUSS, FUSS!

YOU'LL HANG IT IN THE LIVING ROOM, OR I'LL MAKE A TERRIBLE FUSS!
BAH! YOU WIN, FUSS POT! ANYTHING BUT THAT..!

HOW'S THAT?
BAH! CAN'T YOU SEE IT'S UPSIDE-DOWN? AND I WANT TO BE ABLE TO SEE IT FROM WHEREVER I'M SITTING!

AND SO...
I SUPPOSE I'LL HAVE TO DO THE JOB MYSELF! YOU CAN HOLD THE STEPS FOR ME!
Y-YES, FUSS POT..!

THIS IS JUST THE RIGHT SPOT!
OOER! DON'T BANG TOO HARD, FUSS POT..!

HEY! YOU'VE LET GO OF THE STEPS..!
BANG!
CRACK!
YEEOUCH! MY FOOT!
BONK!

OH, DEAR!
OOER! I THINK I KNOW JUST THE SPOT FOR FUSS POT'S PAINTING NOW, MUM..!
HELP!
TOPPLE!
CRASH!

I'M BRINGING FUSS POT IN NOW, DAD!
OKAY, MUM! I'VE JUST FINISHED! CHUCKLE..!

TEE, HEE! THINGS ARE "LOOKING UP" FOR US, NOW WE'LL GET SOME PEACE!
SHE'LL BE ABLE TO LOOK AT HER PAINTING FOR A WHOLE WEEK, NOW! CHUCKLE!
BAH! FUSS! FUSS!

SEEING DOUBLE

See if you can spot three sets of 'twins' among these characters. You need look no further than the antlers.

Answer: 3. (2 and 23, 5 and 21, 9 and 12)